THE HOSPITALITY SUPERVISOR'S SURVIVAL KIT

Cliff Goodwin

Alfred B. Squire III

Elwood Chapman

PEARSON

Prentice
Hall

Upper Saddle River, New Jersey 07458

Library of Congress Cataloging-in-Publication Data

Goodwin, Cliff, 1948–
    Hospitality supervisor's survival kit / Cliff Goodwin, Alfred Squire III.
    Elwood N. Chapman.
        p. cm.
    ISBN 0-13-049846-7
    1. Hospitality industry—Management. I. Squire, Alfred. II. Chapman,
    Elwood N. III. Title.
    TX911.3.M27G663 2005
    647.94'068—dc22

                                                            2004005139

Executive Editor: *Vernon R. Anthony*
Associate Editor: *Marion Gottlieb*
Director of Production and Manufacturing: *Bruce Johnson*
Managing Editor: *Mary Carnis*
Manufacturing Buyer: *Cathleen Petersen*
Production Liaison: *Adele M. Kupchik*
Senior Marketing Manager: *Ryan DeGrote*
Senior Marketing Coordinator: *Elizabeth Farrell*
Marketing Assistant: *Les Roberts*
Design Director: *Cheryl Asherman*
Design Coordinator: *Mary E. Siener*
Cover Design: *Michael L. Ginshing*
Full Service Production/Formatting: *Pine Tree Composition, Inc.*
Editorial Assistant: *Beth Dyke*
Printing and Binding: *Banta Harrisonburg*

Pearson Prentice Hall™ is a trademark of Pearson Education, Inc.
Pearson® is a registered trademark of Pearson plc
Prentice Hall® is a registered trademark of Pearson Education, Inc.

Pearson Education LTD.   Pearson Education Canada, Ltd.
Pearson Education Australia PTY, Limited   Pearson Educación de Mexico, S.A. de C.V.
Pearson Education Singapore, Pte. Ltd   Pearson Education—Japan
Pearson Education North Asia Ltd   Pearson Education Malaysia, Pte. Ltd

10 9 8 7 6 5 4 3 2 1
ISBN 0-13-049846-7

Contents

Creating a Productive Work Climate 62

Helping Your Staff Become a Team 71

PART III LEADING FOR PEAK PERFORMANCE 83

Private Communications 85

Preface

The hospitality industry is a competitive field, and organizations must provide their customers with the best experience possible if they want to beat the competition and stay in business. Supervisors who possess strong leadership skills are key in delivering this excellent customer service. In addition, they are instrumental in creating and maintaining a positive work environment for employees. Organizations that treat their customers better than they treat their employee will not prosper, and supervisors must do for their employees as well as for their customers.

Today the supervisor's job is more complex than ever before. Supervisors must follow federal and state employment laws and enforce health and safety regulations. Additionally, in an increasingly diversified workforce that consists of many different ethnic and age groups, supervisors are expected to demonstrate an appreciation of this diversity, protect everyone's civil rights, utilize everyone's special skills, and train employees when new skills are needed.

The workplace is changing at an unprecedented rate and supervisors are called on to lead their employees through these turbulent times while maintaining high levels of productivity and employee satisfaction. They are expected to problem solve, make decisions, use computers, file reports, conduct meetings, and formulate and execute short- and long-range plans. They are required to assess performance, provide feedback, and counsel their employees. They must interview, orient, and impose discipline when necessary. In light of these expectations, it is important for supervisors to develop skills in human relations, labor and management relations, and customer service to perform their job effectively.

Like any kit, *The Hospitality Supervisor's Survival Kit* contains many "tools." These tools and the concepts presented in this book will help the supervisor be successful in the hospitality industry. The book is divided into five parts: Being a Successful Leader, Creating a Successful Team, Leading for Peak Performance, Getting the Best from Your Team, and Increasing Your Own Opportunities. These parts cover the core concepts of supervision and provide tools vital to effectiveness.

Within these parts many scenarios are presented that are likely to occur as you supervise. They will teach you how to relate to your boss, how to develop your team members for success, and how to build strong and healthy relationships with your employees and upper-level managers. You may see yourself, your employees, and your leaders in the scenarios. It's important to reflect on what you see. If improvements are necessary, make them by using the tools in this supervisor survival kit.

If you are a new supervisor, you are entering a new phase of your career. Not only are you now responsible for your own productivity, you are responsible for the productivity of other people. Your success is contingent on how well you are able to perform through the efforts of your team. Many of the tools presented in this book will help the new supervisor transition into the position.

Many challenges for the supervisor, new or experienced, lie in the "gray areas." These are situations that have no clear answer or there may be more than one right answer. Worse, there may not be any conceivable answer, but supervisors still are expected to deliver. This kit contains the special tools to handle these gray areas.

Typically, hospitality supervisors are not provided with proper training; they are trained with the trial-by-fire method. They are often the "forgotten people" within hospitality organizations. Without training, supervisors are left to learn on their own, and this is a mistake because the job is too complex. Providing training for supervisors is critical to the success of the industry. Effective supervisory skills can be learned, and successful organizations realize this and provide formal training. They know that experience is a good teacher, but it alone is insufficient. This book can be used as a part of this training.

To facilitate student learning, two corresponding guidebooks are available for use with the textbook:

- *Student's Self-Paced Exercise Guide*—Using a variety of experiential exercises, the student study guide facilitates learning by having the students apply the theory and principles found in the textbook within the context of hospitality organizations.

- *The Leader's Guide*—The manual provides guidance to the professional educator in the design, facilitation, and evaluation of a supervisory training course. It contains role-plays, case studies, mini-games, and exam questions. It provides tips on how to use the textbook to deliver training in a semester-long course, appropriate to institutions of higher education, and for in-service training of short duration, like those typically taught within an organization by training professionals.

Supervision is a service role, and supervisors serve people. They serve their bosses, their family, their customers, and their employees. Each of these groups anticipate that the supervisor will support and meet their expectations. We hope that *The Hospitality Supervisor's Survival Kit* will help you to meet the many demands of your job as supervisor.

ACKNOWLEDGMENTS

Many thanks to the reviewers of this book for their insight and invaluable suggestions: Jamal Feerasta, University of Akron; David Hayes, Managing Owner, Clarion Hotel & Conference Center, Lansing, Michigan; Catherine Rabb, Central Piedmont Community College; Carolyn Rigterink, Director of Management Development, HDS Services; Eva Smith, Spartanburg Technical College; and Gary Ward, Scottsdale Community College.

PART I

BEING A SUCCESSFUL LEADER

Being a supervisor in the hospitality industry is a challenging role, especially for new supervisors still learning the skills needed to be an effective leader. In the following chapters we discuss some of the opportunities and challenges today's supervisors and managers face and offer advice on how to make the transition from team member to team leader.

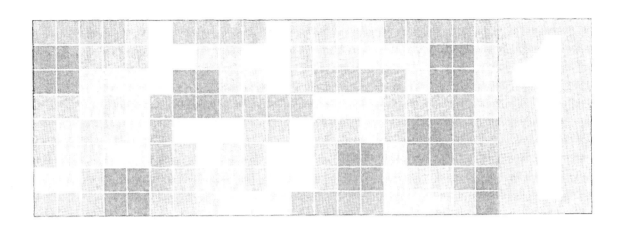

Being a Leader in the Hospitality Industry

The transition into hospitality leadership is an important one. Not only are you choosing a career, you are choosing a lifestyle. You are choosing the manner in which you work and the manner in which you live. There will be tradeoffs.

Your experience as a supervisor can be exciting, challenging, and fulfilling. Or it can be a job you dread. The ideas expressed throughout this book will help you make it a career you enjoy, providing you with the sound principles and guidelines needed to build a rewarding management career. To those of you who are currently a hospitality supervisor and to those of you who plan to become one, we thank you for your efforts and dedicate this edition to your success.

After you have finished reading this chapter, you should be able to

- determine if you should become a hospitality leader,

- know the advantages and disadvantages of taking on a leadership position,

- identify the various relationships that affect or are affected by your job, and

- discover how to spend your time to achieve desired results or performance objective.

THE HOSPITALITY INDUSTRY: OPPORTUNITIES AND CHALLENGES

The hospitality industry caters to people where they work, play, and live. When we eat and when we travel, we patronage establishments that cater to our needs and we seek the comfort of hospitality.

The hospitality industry is an industry of growth and opportunity. Hundreds of billions of dollars are generated in sales. Every year the industry experiences the expansion of successful concepts and the introduction of new ones.

The hospitality industry launches careers. This industry is the best at converting inexperienced and unskilled workers into job/career success stories. It's also one of the best industries for providing advancement from the front line to "the boardroom" to everyone who puts forth the effort to excel. Outside the government, no industry employs as many people as the hospitality industry. Nearly everyone knows someone who has worked or is currently working in the hospitality industry. Chances are, you are reading this book because you are in this industry and want to improve your career opportunities.

The hospitality industry resonates with creative ideas. The industry continues to reinvent itself with creative cuisines, building designs, and service amenities. Entrepreneurs are constantly creating new directions to expand the industry.

Growth, competition, change, creativity, and retention, whether good or bad, are the product of the efforts of our industry leaders. The skills and abilities of leadership determine the success or failure of companies.

Why is it that certain companies prevail when other companies fail in the same market? What determines the success of one company over its nearly identical competitor? Why do certain companies continually exceed investors' expectations? Why do certain individuals excel in their management careers while others stagnate? Each of these questions can be answered by examining the topic of leadership.

Effective leaders are desperately needed in the hospitality industry. Those who practice sound leadership principles will earn opportunities for advancement. Your leadership skills will determine whether you grow and prosper in the industry or find frustration and failure.

SHOULD YOU BECOME A LEADER IN HOSPITALITY?

There are many reasons people want to become hospitality leaders; the following examples illustrate a few.

- Marcello dreams of being in charge of his own restaurant. As he scrubs the encrusted pots from this afternoon's lunch, he ponders how he can go from the dishroom to the boardroom.

- Pam sits in her car outside of her parents' home, crying. The job market has not been kind to new graduates, especially graduates who lack management experience.

- Sharlonda is not happy. She is tired of doing other team members' jobs, tired of working for bosses who don't know how to do their job. Sharlonda thinks if she was in charge, she could do a better job than her boss.

- Manuel has been happy as a short-order chef for three years. Yesterday he was offered a position as night supervisor at a substantial increase in pay. Should he accept the challenge?

- During John's performance review he was told he was doing a good job. He was also told he could not make any more money in his hourly position. John can choose to accept the limits that have been placed on him in his current position or seek a new job.

Management Positions and Leadership Abilities

Being a supervisor means you are responsible for the success of your business. By definition, **management is getting things done within an organization through other people.** This means

- guiding people's efforts toward organizational objectives;

- inspiring, communicating, planning, organizing, controlling, and evaluating; and

- setting goals and moving team members toward them.

If you are ready to accept responsibility for the people you lead, leadership is right for you.

How important are people to you? The hospitality industry caters to the needs of people. Your ability to understand, nurture, and maintain relationships creates the foundation for your success.

You must be a servant, confidante, personnel director, counselor, teacher, student, disciplinarian, marketer, coach, expert, strategist, and, at times, a sociologist, psychologist, and a mind reader to be a successful leader.

You must learn to work constructively with people and accept people who irritate, frustrate, disappoint, and hurt you. You must develop interpersonal or people skills, such as active listening. You must also develop strong written and verbal communication skills.

You must familiarize yourself with employment laws such as Title VII of the Civil Rights Act of 1964 as well. This law is important for all supervisors because it pertains to the civil rights of your team members. In addition, you must be receptive to assist new team members from diverse cultures.

You also must have a great deal of patience, perception, and compassion. In other words, you must like people—all kinds of people. You can't fake it. People will know if you try to fool them, just as you know when people are not being forthright with you.

If people are truly important to you, building lasting relationships with those you supervise can be highly rewarding—sometimes more rewarding than the money you make. Building mutually satisfying relationships with others in and out of your organization is a key component to effective leadership.

If you are ready to accept the responsibility of helping the members of your staff achieve and be recognized for their success, the responsibility of leadership is right for you.

To be a successful leader in the hospitality industry, you have to be willing to train and develop the people you lead. As a leader, having the ability to perform tasks will never be as important as having the ability to train and develop others to do those same tasks. In your role as a supervisor, you no longer have to be the best worker. Focus on being the best coach. It is no longer your responsibility to be a star performer. It is your job to be a star creator. Focusing your efforts on educating, enabling, and empowering the stars on your team is your job. Take pride in knowing you helped others perform better.

How strong is your drive to help others be better? Are you willing to do whatever is necessary to help others be successful? Your success is predicated by the success of your team. Commit yourself to helping your staff be successful and your efforts will create opportunities for you. If you can become a superior supervisor, more responsible management positions will be open to you. In fact, you will be able to go as far as your ambition and leadership skills will take you.

If you prefer to plan and organize work, the responsibility of leadership is right for you.

Do you consider yourself a good planner? Are you an organizer? Can you multitask? In the hospitality industry you, as a supervisor, must have the ability to function on three levels:

Level One: Your Primary Position

You must focus on excelling in your primary position. Directing the activities of your daily operations and taking care of your personnel must be your priority. This means training and developing your team and managing daily activities while planning future events.

Level Two: Your Role as a Supportive Company Team Player

Your position will affect the function of other departments in your company. Other people will depend on you to aid them in performing their jobs. Many of these departments, such as payroll, accounting, and human resources, will provide support or services to you. In order for these departments to effectively assist you, you must complete specific tasks for them. Attending meetings, completing administrative paperwork, and performing special assignments are among the things that you will be asked to do. Working beyond the core responsibilities of your primary position is required of you as a company team player.

Level Three: Your Role in the Hospitality Industry and Your Community

The further you rise on the leadership ladder, the more prudent it will be for you to contribute back to the hospitality industry as well as your community through mentoring and volunteer work. The time you spend advancing the interests and causes of the industry and your community will prove worthy to yourself, your career, your business, your industry, and your community.

Managing the demands of your time and prioritizing your assignments will require planning. Supervisors must prepare and implement plans to organize their time and complete their assignments. You will need to determine how to use your time to achieve your performance objectives. You will need to spend time discovering, designing, developing, delegating, and doing the tasks required to aid you in being a successful supervisor and achieving your performance objectives.

If you are willing to grow in your abilities as a leader, a position in leadership is right for you.

A hospitality supervisor, more than anything else, is a leader. He or she must set the tempo, provide the inspiration, and sometimes nurse the team members along, as well as exercise harsh discipline and hand out constructive feedback. It is a constant balancing act to keep the team spirit of the department alive. Although some people seem to have natural leadership ability, most supervisors have had to develop their skills through training, experience, and reflection on their experiences. Don't worry about whether you have been able to demonstrate your leadership yet; it's the desire that counts. If you feel you have the potential, look ahead with confidence to your role as a supervisor. Opportunities to demonstrate your leadership will come later.

Advantages of Leading Others

If you have never been a leader, it may be difficult to predict how you will react or perform. If you have the slightest interest in finding out what your chances are, why not try? Start preparing now and accept the first opportunity that presents itself. Here are some advantages to consider.

1. Hospitality is a growth industry and opportunities abound. One out of every nine team member positions is a supervisory or management position. There is room for you. You can literally go from the dishroom to the boardroom, from making salads to creating visions, and from stocking products to stock options. The opportunity to move up is nearly always present for those who are willing to plan ahead and prepare. The hospitality industry is booming with opportunities due to growth and expansion, and opportunities for advancement up the corporate ladder is therefore increasing. Those who develop their leadership abilities will gain opportunities to move into upper managerial positions. You are a decision away from your next position. Decide what position you want, prepare yourself for that position, and take advantage of the opportunities to get that position.

2. Becoming a first line supervisor is often a good way to achieve a better salary and standard of living. You will deserve higher salary because, as an effective leader, you will increase the productivity and profitability of your organization.

3. Supervisors often have greater opportunities to participate in company training. Take every opportunity to learn new skills. Supervisors are often given the opportunity to attend seminars on leadership, team dynamics, or technical areas like inventory control, customer service, sales, human resources, and quality assurance.

4. Supervisors are usually well informed on organizational issues. They are members of the management team. They attend meetings, receive written reports and communications, and are often consulted by upper levels. They interact with other supervisors and deal with a wide variety of challenges. The supervisor's job is a challenging one, but keep in mind that research shows that challenging work is a powerful motivator for most people.

5. Supervisors are in an ideal position to contribute to the growth and development of those they supervise. The supervisor is the team member's link to opportunities within the organization. The effective supervisor trains and develops her or his team in order to take advantage of these opportunities. Employees who work for effective supervisors are more likely to be promoted than do those who report to ineffective supervisors. Success begets success.

6. Supervisors are more mobile than workers. As a hospitality supervisor you will find it easier to advance in your career within your company or take advantages of other opportunities in the industry because you will gain additional knowledge and experience and demonstrated leadership skills.

Disadvantages of Leading Others

In addition to the many advantages in becoming a leader, there are disadvantages. Think about them before making a final commitment.

1. Problem employees can be difficult. As a team member, you have already noticed that some co-workers have unusual behavior patterns that cause problems for their supervisors. Handling confrontations, working with grievances, and conducting corrective interviews can be traumatic for some people. Supervisors have sometimes found themselves in the middle of complex human problems that seem to have no possible solution.

2. Expect to be more alone as a supervisor. Successful supervisors—even team leaders—must isolate themselves to some extent from the team members they supervise. It can be difficult to be a supervisor and a close friend at the same time. You must frequently back away when you might rather be a part of the group. You may be asked to withhold confidential information from your team members until an official announcement is made. As a member of the management team, your team members may perceive you as being one of "them" and not one of "us." You will feel this isolation most when you make an unpopular decision and the people you supervise let you know you are on opposite sides. It is an unreasonable expectation to think that you can please everyone all the time.

3. You may not receive constant reinforcement from your own supervisor. Management people usually treat other supervisors differently from the way supervisors treat their team members. As a supervisor, you will be expected to support and protect your team members at all times. You must give them day-to-day security and constant personal attention. Do not, however, expect this same treatment from your manager. Because you are a supervisor, you are expected to be stronger, so your manager may not feel the same need to reinforce you. He or she will take it for granted that you will provide your own personal confidence and self-motivation.

4. You may have to change your behavior more than you expect. Becoming a supervisor for the first time may become one of the most important things to happen to you in your lifetime. It can be a bigger transition than people expect. In becoming a supervisor, you lay your career and reputation on the line; if you fail, your adjustment to a lower level can be brutally difficult and often impossible. The change requires realigning your thinking because your whole approach to your career must be different. Your daily routine, your human relationships, and your self-concept may have to change. To underestimate the degree of change you might have to make could cause you to fail as a supervisor.

5. A position as a supervisor will mean longer hours without overtime pay because supervisory positions are generally salaried. It also may mean taking extra work home with you. You may be asked to attend seminars on your own time. You will be expected to manage your time and the time of others. Many deadlines can only be met with appropriate planning and time management techniques. You may not be paid extra for the time this planning takes. Often, a supervisor's schedule is so tight during the regular working day that he or she might typically take work home. This extra work can cut into family time. Such is the price for those who wish to lead.

6. High productivity and high quality standards are more important today than they were during the last decade. One of your challenges will be to gain higher quality standards and greater production with fewer people. These demands will increase the pressure on supervisors to learn new technology and approaches in workflow and job design. Your success will depend on the work of your direct reports. As a supervisor you are directly accountable for the productivity of those reporting to you.

7. Your skills as a supervisor may need to be developed. Often, the best and most capable technician may be given a promotion to supervisor. Even though technical skills are important, other skills are needed too. As mentioned earlier, you will need interpersonal and leadership skills as well as time management abilities.

THE HOSPITALITY SUPERVISOR

The next time you visit your favorite restaurant, notice what the leaders are doing. You may see that some are doing the exact same work of the team members who are not supervisors. This is acceptable when they are in the midst of training someone. Maybe (and we do mean maybe) it is acceptable during a peak time; however, it is counterproductive. The hospitality industry is notorious for making the supervisor position a glorified team member or honorary worker position. This image of the supervisor has devalued the significance of this position and has falsely altered the opinions of people for what this industry has to offer. This is a shame.

Changes in the hospitality industry during the last few years have, without question, focused more attention on the hospitality supervisor—the man or woman who is willing to assume the growing responsibility of leading a food operations or lodging establishment to greater productivity. It may have been easier to become a supervisor and survive in the past because the rules were less complicated and the job had fewer responsibilities. It was more like playing ball in the minor leagues. Today, being a hospitality supervisor is a major league job. The challenge is greater, but so are the rewards.

The supervisor is a key player in the management hierarchy. Due to competition for workers and the growth of the industry, the importance of the role of the hospitality supervisor has increased dramatically. The obvious reason is that many restaurant and lodging establishments' success depends on how much the hospitality supervisor position is willing to bear.

The Stress of Supervision

If you are a supervisor in hospitality, take a moment now to list some of the pressures you face each day.

As you study your list, you will see that your pressures come from a wide variety of sources. Some pressures are more serious than others, but serious or not, they all add up and can produce distress for the supervisor. Are these pressures too costly for you personally?

Some believe that becoming a leader is injurious to one's physical and mental health because of excessive pressures. This is a myth. Supervisors, in general, are as healthy as those not in management. The supervisor can learn to deal with organizational pressures just as the politician must deal with public pressures. Certainly the job may tax your nervous system a little more than some other kinds of work, and the emotional and mental strain may be greater in some organizations than in others. Every job has its own special demands. The solution, of course, is to handle the job without letting it become too much of a strain. Special courses teach strategies for dealing with stress. Take advantage of any training or help the company provides. You can learn how to manage your stress.

Some individuals who are highly self-motivated apply pressure to themselves by setting difficult goals. Unrealistic goals can add to your stress.

Let's look at an example of one individual who wanted the challenge and involvement of a supervisory role.

Ezra is thinking about taking a promotion to supervisor of the front desk. He has always prided himself as one of the best employees in his department. His immediate supervisor recognizes his contributions and has offered him the opportunity to move into management. Should he take it or not is the question that has been occupying his mind recently.

Ezra realizes that as a supervisor he will need to use skills that he may not fully possess at this time. Sure, he is highly skilled at doing his current job. He has been trained very well, and he is a quick learner. These, however, are not the same skills he will use as a supervisor. He will be expected to hire (or fire), administer performance appraisals, create and maintain a motivating environment, listen to his employees, solve problems, manage change, train and develop his team, fill out reports, and interact with other managers in meetings. Is he up to the challenge? He wonders. He is approaching his new opportunity with an excellent attitude.

He decides to talk with Sheila, a highly effective, well-respected, supervisor, to gain her thoughts.

More Responsibility, Less Support

Today more responsibility has fallen on the shoulders of the hospitality supervisor. He or she must play a larger part in the operations with less support. In addition, hospitality supervisors must deal with a wide assortment of new factors:

- a more culturally diverse work team,

- an environment that produces high turnover among team members,

- flex scheduling, which may mean molding an operations team out of a mix of full-time and part-time workers,

- dealing with team members on issues of sexual harassment, childcare, and absenteeism,

- ■ managing a progressively demanding clientele,

- ■ constant changes in procedures and systems, and

- ■ incorporating new technologies into administrative systems.

Advantages of Being on the Front Line

There are some advantages to being a hospitality supervisor on the front lines. Many supervisors appreciate the fast-paced environment. They love being in the thick of things, performing activities that will make them victorious over their competition. By being on the front line, you are able to affect controllables. You can make decisions while observing and directing the activities of your department. You also are able to observe and affect the performance of your staff based on personal observations. Finally, when appropriate, you are able to assist in the execution of excellent service by contributing your own efforts.

The industry shift to more supervisors working on the front line has produced various changes in the scope of work for the hospitality supervisor:

- ■ More decisions are being made at the operations level.

- ■ Effective supervisors are easier to spot and will receive "first call" on promotional possibilities.

- ■ Women and minorities who excel discover that the so-called glass ceiling is less apt to exist in their organizations.

- ■ Hospitality supervisors have more autonomy and are expected to run their operations as if they own the business.

- ■ Hospitality supervisors are encouraged to operate with more authority while expecting to be held accountable.

- ■ Hospitality supervisors receive more advance training.

Team members who aspire to become supervisors will be expected to demonstrate their abilities with more force and enthusiasm. Not only will their personal performance and contribution to the higher performance of others be evaluated, management also will evaluate how prepared they are to assume the role of the supervisor. Obviously, being accepted as a new supervisor will be more of an achievement in the future than it has been in the past.

YOUR USE OF AUTHORITY

A supervisory position gives you the authority to direct and affect the work of others. Initially, your direct reports will respond to you because of your position. You are their boss.

More important, they will respond to your leadership. You have the ability to alter, positively or negatively, how people perceive and respond to you. Utilize the full scope of your authority to establish yourself, but be cautious in how you use your authority; never allow your authority to become abusive.

The following letters reflect what can happen if you use this power wisely or abuse it.

THE TALE OF TWO LETTERS

Dear Team,

Thank you!

It is great to work here!

Every day I have the honor of working with some of the greatest team members in the industry.

We get to do what we do best every day: help each other take care of our customers. It is great to be on this team. We've worked hard to get to this point and every day we strive to get a little better.

Each day we learn and grow from our experience. You work in a place where you are trained and praised for what you do.

It's amazing what we accomplish by working together. None of us can do everything, but all of us can do something. Each of you contributing your best makes all of us successful. You are the reason "we" make a difference to our customers. You're the reason working here is so rewarding.

I am committed to your success and making sure you perform your best. You can count on me just like I rely on you. We'll take care of each other. My performance is only as good as your performance.

I will work hard to make you better.

Thank you for making this a great place to work.

Truly Appreciative,

Your Supervisor

Dear Supervisor,

You're fired.

Each time one of us quits, we are firing you.

Some of us are going to go work someplace else. When they ask why we quit, we'll make something up. We'll say something that sounds legit. Don't worry; we won't tell the truth. No one will ever know that we are quitting you.

Some of us are quitting but we're going to stay. We will report to work every day. We'll refuse to work to our capacity. We'll take our time and won't care about accuracy. You didn't notice us when we were working. Perhaps you will notice when we start shirking. We'll see what happens when your sales decline.

Maybe you'll learn and change your ways. If you don't, you won't stay.

Supervisor, you have forgotten that you work for us. You have forgotten what it was like when you were us.

You tell us we haven't done "our time."

Had you taken care of us, we would have given you a raise. But you fail to give us our deserving praise.

Now we are giving you your "walking papers."

See ya, Supervisor, it's time to replace you.

Formerly Yours,

Your Ex-Team Members

Any worthwhile endeavor takes hard work, dedication, continuous learning, and an eager willingness to take on challenges. The role of the hospitality supervisor is a worthwhile endeavor to be sure, one worthy of your consideration and attention. Effective supervisors and leaders exhibit similar behaviors. The following is a listing of dos and don'ts. Practice the behaviors found in the do list and minimize the use of the don'ts and your chances for success as a supervisor will be greatly increased.

DOS AND DON'TS: TIPS ON TECHNIQUES	
DOS	**DON'TS**
DO create opportunities for your team members to get to know you. Build trust and respect through meaningful work.	**DON'T** issue edicts demanding trust and respect from your team. Neither of these items can be forced; they must be earned.
DO give time to your team. They need your guidance and support. They need you.	**DON'T** manage through memos. Memos should be used when information needs to be widely dispersed or documented.
DO encourage open and honest communications.	**DON'T** automatically assume everything you hear is accurate. Validate the information, especially when you question the source.
DO pay attention to what is being said (and not said).	**DON'T** select individuals to dominate your time.
DO make sure people know it is okay to make mistakes while learning.	**DON'T** treat people like children when they make mistakes.
DO see that everyone has a chance to improve their performance to a known standard.	**DON'T** ignore performance or behavior that's not right.
DO help your team know the vision, strategies, and tactics that help them to successfully achieve your goals.	**DON'T** allow select participation. Everyone must be working toward your goals.
DO make sure the group has what it needs to be successful (i.e., materials, time, tools, etc.).	**DON'T** fail to plan.
DO understand each individuals' needs as well as team needs.	**DON'T** allow individuals to compromise the team.
DO provide the group with feedback on their accomplishments as well as their challenges.	**DON'T** forget to celebrate their achievements and train their shortcomings.
DO focus on the process—how things are done, how information is gathered, how decisions are made, and so on.	**DON'T** ignore conflict. Make sure you focus on the problems and not the personalities. Help team members understand the consequences of their behavior by providing open, honest feedback when they ask for it, and, more important, when they don't.
DO help people develop communication and team skills.	**DON'T** create dependency on one person.

CONCLUSION

Effective leaders are desperately needed in the hospitality industry. Those who practice sound leadership principles will earn opportunities for advancement. The ideas expressed throughout this book will help you make it a career you enjoy, providing you with the sound principles and guidelines needed to build a rewarding management career. The supervisor is a key player in the management hierarchy. A supervisory position gives you the authority to direct and affect the work of others.

DISCUSSION QUESTIONS

1. How can being a hospitality supervisor affect your standard of living?

2. Why is it more important to have the ability to teach people how to perform a given task rather than perform the task for them?

3. How should you spend your time to achieve performance objectives?

4. Explain how leadership in the hospitality industry impacts industry growth, competition, change, creativity, and retention.

5. Looking at the letters on page 13, explain why other team members quit your previous employer.

6. Describe the job of your supervisor.

7. What Dos and Don'ts are most applicable to your situation right now?

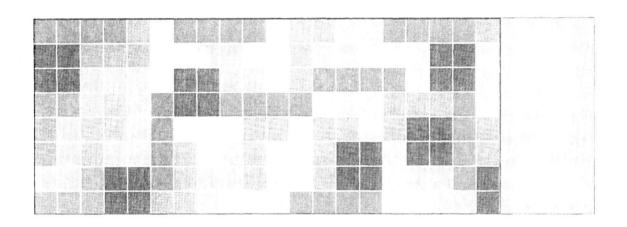

Guidelines for the New Supervisor

After you have finished reading this chapter, you should be able to

- discuss the prior-image issue faced by supervisors promoted internally,
- talk about strategies to use to become a successful new supervisor,
- discuss goals a new supervisor should have, and
- explain the importance of balancing home and career responsibilities.

MAKING THE TRANSITION FROM PEER TO SUPERVISOR

Harry and Sally have just become supervisors for the same organization and have similar personal goals and job experiences. Their supervisory appointments, however, occurred under different circumstances.

Harry knew about his promotion three months in advance. He was able to prepare for his new responsibilities by taking a supervisor course at a nearby community college, reading about management, and working closely as an understudy to the person he was to replace. This preparation allowed a smooth transition for both Harry and the organization. Sally, on the other hand, was a regular team member one day and a supervisor the next. Unlike Harry, who was groomed for his new role, Sally became an "instant supervisor" with almost no opportunity to prepare.

Why didn't Sally receive the same training and preparation time as Harry? The answer is simple: In the changing world of hospitality, management cannot always predict supervisory vacancies caused by resignations, transfers, and promotions. Sudden growth also may cause the demand for supervisors to be greater than the supply. Consequently, management is often forced to fill slots quickly. Remarks like the following are being made somewhere in the hospitality industry every day:

- I realize, Palmer, that you have been with us for only three months and haven't had supervisory experience, but because of an emergency, we want you to take over managing convention sales tomorrow morning.

- It may come as a shock, Susan, because we haven't had a chance to groom you as a team leader, but we'd rather give you the opportunity than to bring in an outsider.

- Remember when you came to work, Sam? You said you wanted to be a supervisor within a year. Well, you have made it ahead of schedule. Drop by my office later, and we will talk about salary and other details.

Men and women of all ages take their first step up the management ladder without preparation.

- Last year Donna served tables. Now she manages servers—her former peers.
- Steven has been on staff a long time. He enjoys coming to work. He loves working in sales and catering with his friends. Tomorrow he will be named the new supervisor.
- George, the new supervisor, was fired after only two months. He trusted the wrong team member for guidance.

No matter what your age, education, or experience, you can't predict what opportunities will occur. You can't anticipate when your supervisor will leave or when some other supervisory opening will occur. Even in periods of recession, opportunities surface.

HANDLING AN INTERNAL PROMOTION

Typically, new supervisors are promoted into their first supervisory position from a nonsupervisory job within the same organization. The new supervisor may remain within the same department or be transferred to another department. In either case, you will have a challenging experience ahead of you. Your new position grants you respect. Your behavior determines whether you keep it.

You are going to have to help people learn how to treat you in your new role. The best way for them to learn is for you to show them respect and understanding. They have concerns just like you and are wondering about the same things:

- How do I act around you now that you're a supervisor?

- What can we do together at work? After work?

- What can we talk about?

Teaching people how to treat you involves carrying yourself in a professional manner and using sensitive interpersonal skills.

The Prior-Image Issue

Before your promotion to supervisor you were perhaps "one of the guys." You belonged to the group. You were their peer, one of them. You may have behaved in ways that were counterproductive to the organization. For example, you may have said some negative things or complained about your supervisor or upper management, or perhaps you called in sick when you were not. Your fellow team members will remember your past behavior. You may even find yourself having to discipline one of your employees for exhibiting a behavior that you exhibited before your promotion to supervisor. You may be reminded of this fact, and the individual may challenge your motives for imposing discipline. If challenged for this reason, focus your discussion on the inappropriate behavior and provide reasons why it must change. You may find it helpful to acknowledge the fact that you used to do some inappropriate things but you have changed.

Overcoming your prior image may be a challenge, but it is possible. Remember, too, that you have done many things that contributed to the effectiveness of your department. They are why you were promoted. Your former workmates will also remember your past contributions. This will prove to be beneficial in your transition.

You shouldn't forget your past. Cherish the accomplishments that fill you with pride; you will need to recall these moments when you're faced with challenges or when feeling ineffective in your new role. You are going to face many crossroads in your future; summoning strength from your past will prove invaluable. Leave your ineffective behaviors behind you and take what you have learned from your life lessons into your future.

Understand that you have many more life lessons to experience as well. It is inevitable and necessary that these lessons occur. Many will be learned vicariously through others' experiences, such as lessons from mentors, videos, and this book. Other lessons will be learned from your own experiences. Some experiences will fill you with pride. Others will make you want to cry. There is something to learn in every achievement and every mistake. Learn to reflect on your past experiences. Guided reflection is the foundation of learning. We must learn from our past experiences and use what we learn to become more effective in the future. Repeating the same old mistakes time and again will happen to you if you refuse to analyze and learn from your experiences.

Handling an External Promotion

Many assumptions will be made about you before you report to work. Some of them will be accurate, others will not. Your first appearance on the job will confirm some of those assumptions. If possible, visit the workplace before the announcement of your appointment. Get to know how your new organization operates. If your organization is a restaurant, eat there; if it's a hotel, stay there. Use room service; experience what customers experience. This will aid you in understanding the particulars of your job, the dynamics of your team, and areas requiring your attention.

Top Ten Things to Do as a New Supervisor

As a new supervisor, you should accomplish the following during the first few weeks:

1. **Introduce yourself to your direct reports.** Allow you and your team time to get to know one another. Provide them with some personal information (e.g., explain your thoughts about leadership and about how you should lead others). You may answer personal questions, such as, Are you married? Do you have children? Where did you grow up? What are some of your interests or hobbies? Self-disclosure such as this can help team members see you as a person, not just as a supervisor. Show interest in them as people. Spend a few minutes each day taking with each one of your employees.

   Everyone will be wondering how receptive and available you will be to them. The most important thing you can do right now is *listen*. Schedule one-on-one meetings with your immediate staff and listen. Attend meetings and listen. Meet with your peers, ask questions, and listen. When people in leadership positions in your organization speak, listen. When customers speak, listen. When team members speak, listen. Not everything you hear will be valid, but everything you hear will need to be heard. Seek information through conversations. Be cautious, however, because certain individuals with want to dominate your time. Remember to take notes and try to listen to what is not being said as well as to what is said.

2. **Ask questions and listen to advice.** Keep in mind that your employees and fellow supervisors can often assist you in making your transition. Collectively they know a whole lot more about the organization than you. Information is power. Get as much of it as possible from as many sources as possible. Do not hesitate to ask for help when confronted with a problem you do not know how to handle.

3. **Think like management.** Make some progress in the direction of becoming a solid member of the management team. Start the process by thinking like a supervisor rather than a team member. Do not fall into the trap of criticizing management openly to your team members; work as a member of management to correct problems and do so with a spirit of unity and teamwork.

4. **Stay positive.** No matter how you feel on the inside, stay positive and appear confident on the outside; smile and be friendly. Remain visible, walk about, and do not retreat to your office.

5. **Do not form alliances.** Maintain a neutral stance in your assessment of everyone.

6. **Document your observations.** Note things you like and things that will need improvements.

7. **Review files.** Documents are kept for a reason. Read files to find out the history of your operation and your team members.

8. **Notice your environment.** How are workspaces decorated? You can learn a great deal about the workplace and the people from the aesthetics of your work environment. Notice personal artifacts and awards, but don't snoop—observe.

9. **Notice how people are dressed.** Make sure you dress appropriately; never dress below your position.

10. **Do not make a lot of changes.** Respect the past. Your team may need to change some things, but they obviously did many things correctly. Too many initial changes may undermine your relationship with them. The organization existed before your arrival. Respect this fact by not announcing that there are going to be major changes. Spend time gathering impressions and data on current operations. This will help identify areas that need improvement, but move slowly at first. Remember that you do not have a track record yet and trust in you may be low. Your wanting to change things without understanding the operations fully may be interpreted as arrogance. Sudden change scares many people. Unless management demands immediate changes, it is best to get used to the way the department operates before introducing major innovations. When you are ready to make changes, explain them to the people who will be affected by them. And remember, people are more motivated to make changes when they have been involved in the planning of that change.

Later, you can attempt to accomplish results that are more dramatic. If the first steps have been successful, your future goals are attainable. The willingness of your team members to follow you rests on your track record. The way you pace yourself during the first few weeks will have an impact on determining your long-range success or failure.

Let's look at an example of what a new supervisor should do.

After two years of waiting, Ron finally was promoted to a supervisor position with Meals On A Run restaurants. He was responsible for the morning rush hour, working with seven full-time team members. He began with great enthusiasm, by encouraging and spending time with team members. By letting them work in the manner they were accustomed to working, Ron was able to observe their productivity. He made notes to himself on things he felt they performed well and on things that could be approved upon. One by one, Ron sat down with each team member.

Ron learned a lot from these meetings. He was apprised of ideas team members had to make their jobs better, what frustrated them, and what they expected of him. Ron also was able to share his expectation and goals for the restaurant with his team members. Ron expressed that he depended on and expected each team member to aid him in making them successful.

Knowing he was new, Ron called managers at other units to solicit information and bounce ideas off them concerning how he could better run his operations. Ron also spent time with customers, learning more of what they thought of the restaurant.

Armed with knowledge from his team members, his customers, and his peers, Ron adopted ideas from all three groups and developed a strategic plan. After gaining insight from his supervisor, Ron went to work putting his plan into action. Within a year, the results of Ron's efforts were explosive. The restaurant sales, customers' satisfaction ratings, and team member retention reached all-time highs. Ron received recognition from the corporate office and was asked to share how he achieved such great numbers. Ron responded that he listened and involved his team members; he responded to the needs of his customers; he sought assistance from his peers and his boss; and, most important, he credited his team for his success.

More Strategies for New Supervisors

To help you survive during your first few weeks as a supervisor, try these additional suggestions along with the Top Ten List presented earlier. They can make the difference between a sound, easy transition and a needlessly difficult one. These suggestions may get you through the initial period when people's reactions to you may be the most critical.

Use Your New Power in a Sensitive Manner

You may think it can't happen to you, but sudden authority has a strange way of inflating your feelings of self-importance. Guard against this danger by neutralizing your new power with a strong dose of humility. Keep reminding yourself that you are basically the same person you were before. You must now succeed through the efforts of others; do not abuse your new authority and create hostility in those who now must look to you for leadership.

Naturally, you will want to satisfy your superiors during your first few weeks because you must earn their support. In doing so, however, be sure to protect those who work in your department. Do not pass on to your people the sudden pressures you feel from above. You must act as a buffer and keep your frustrations and disappointments to yourself if you are to keep a smoothly operating, productive department. Your job is to make the work of those in your department easier, not harder.

Be Patient with Yourself

Your first days as a supervisor may be hectic. You will face paperwork and deadlines you didn't expect, meetings that will gobble up your time, and problems you didn't anticipate. At the same time, you may become impatient because you want to try new things right away. Try to relax. You may wish to confide in a fellow supervisor or with your supervisor. Support from others you trust can help you deal effectively with change.

Stay in Close Contact with All Team Members

The temptation to please management by increasing productivity may cause you to be less sensitive to the people in your department and their problems. This insensitivity is a serious mistake. Despite all your pressing new responsibilities, it is important that you take time to make personal, positive contacts with each team member in the department during your first few weeks as their supervisor, regardless of whether you were promoted from within the department or brought in from outside. These contacts can be accomplished through brief stand-up conversations, coffee-break talks, or invitations to talk things over, depending on the number of team members, the time available, and other circumstances. Hold regularly scheduled team meetings where your team members can give and receive new information or instruction on operational issues as well. The purpose of each contact is to let each team member know that you appreciate that person as an individual. It is your responsibility to initiate the contact and build the relationship.

Get Yourself Oriented

Try to get the lay of the land as quickly as possible. Your position of leadership entails certain written and unwritten agreements or ground rules of operation. Learn the rules and regulations. Ask the Human Resources Department, if your organization has one, for assistance in learning company policies and procedures. Read the team member handbook if one exists and take notes.

Spend Time with Your Boss

Learn the history of your role and your boss's expectations of someone in your role. Learn his or her priorities, and remember, take notes!

To help find out what your manager's expectations are, ask the following questions:

- Are you about to encounter some sensitive human relations situations you need to know about in advance?
- Will you be inheriting a problem team member?
- Do any special legal or safety precautions require your attention?

■ Does your leadership style differ significantly from that of your predecessor?

■ Should you be apprised of some informal reports or unusual protocol?

Some new supervisors make a list of questions similar to those just given so that they can get answers in advance and avoid unnecessary initial mistakes. You hope answers to such questions will come automatically from your new superior before or shortly after you make your transition, but do not depend on it. You may have to uncover the problems and dig up some answers on your own.

Even if you do an outstanding job of learning which hurdles to jump and which to avoid, your position will likely have other pitfalls to guard against. It is one thing to learn theory to prepare for leadership, but it's quite another to put that knowledge into practice. No matter how much formal preparation you receive in advance, your first few weeks are critical. If at all possible, begin on the right foot. Here are some tips to follow:

■ Introduce yourself to your team—disclose a little personal information (e.g., how you like to lead, your preferred style of leadership, etc.).

■ Don't be hasty to change things, even if obvious improvements are necessary.

Save Some Planning Time

The hustle and bustle of being a new supervisor may cause you to spin your wheels and try to operate without a plan. You might solve one problem only to discover that a problem having a much higher priority has been neglected. Take the time to think and plan. Evaluate yourself and your performance on a day-to-day basis. If you cannot find any time for planning while you are on the job, do it at home—it's that important.

Redefine Your Workplace Friendships

It is possible that some of your close on-the-job friends will try to capitalize on a previous personal relationship now that you are a supervisor. In other words, they may seek preferential treatment. Do not permit this manipulation. Your first responsibility as a supervisor is to keep all relationships with your people fair and equal. If you violate this principle at the beginning, you will jeopardize the respect and confidence you receive from your other team members.

Previous co-workers with whom you have mature friendships will recognize your new responsibilities and will not expect favoritism. These friendships can continue to be close, although both parties may need to redefine their relationship and expend additional energy to keep it in balance. As you adjust to these situations, new standards of integrity on your part may be necessary. Matters such as confidentiality (keeping management matters to yourself), self-control, and personal adherence to company rules will come into play.

Let Your Team Members Help You

Many people are motivated by involvement. Involve your team members in planning, decision making, and problem solving. Some of your team members may know more about your department than you do. Ask their advice and accept it.

Involve them in as many decisions as possible, especially those decisions that will affect their work routine. You need their help, especially at the beginning.

Adopt a Learning Attitude

As a supervisor, do not become so preoccupied with pleasing everyone that you neglect your education. Do not hesitate to ask necessary questions of your superiors, fellow supervisors, and knowledgeable team members; continue to read and study this book (it will help after you become a supervisor); and enroll in any available outside courses that can offer important direction to your success. For example, if you discover that your new role is putting extra demands on you in a specific area, such as attracting new business through local marketing initiatives, study these skills on the outside while you are performing inside. Lifelong learning is necessary in our modern world. Take the opportunity to learn new skills when you can; do not become obsolete.

BALANCING CAREER AND HOME

New supervisors have two important reasons for learning how to balance home and career effectively. The first reason is to prosper as supervisors, and the second is to teach their team members to do the same. A healthy balance is most important and perhaps most difficult in a single-parent family. Working at work and working at home leave little time for other important activities. Here are four tips to assist you in achieving balance:

■ Apply some of the techniques you learn in this book both at work and at home. Remember that home can be a good, safe place to practice newly acquired techniques of leadership.

■ Demonstrate to your team members and superiors that you know how to balance home and career by not sacrificing one for the other. Stresses at work can cause stress at home and vice versa. It can be difficult to keep one from spilling over into the other.

■ Use your time off to catch up on home responsibilities and enjoy a few leisure activities so that you return to work refresh and organized.

■ Allocate some quiet time to plan your daily activities.

DECIDE TO BE A PROFESSIONAL

When you first become a supervisor, be careful not to create more problems than you solve. Move in with confidence and enthusiasm, but keep your eyes open, don't destroy previous relationships, and build new ones. Create a climate of excitement, but don't sacrifice your long-range goals for immediate gains. Remember that it is easier to win popularity than to achieve respect. The management ladder has many rungs; if you don't make a smooth transition to the first one, you may never climb the others.

One way to be happy as a supervisor is to be effective. Personal pride will come after you feel comfortable with your new role. Recognition from both your team members and superiors will signal your arrival.

QUALITY OF YOUR WORK LIFE	QUALITY OF YOUR HOME LIFE
Become more focused on achieving your goals.	Do your chores, then play.
Learn techniques that will make you more effective as a supervisor.	Talk about your work with your family.
Avoid procrastination.	Plan your personal life.
Have a positive attitude that others will want to model.	Welcome variety into your life and keep a sense of humor.
Consistently maintain standards of performance without having to be at work all the time.	Enjoy the companionship of your loved ones.
Position yourself for success.	Position yourself for happiness.

CONCLUSION

Typically, new supervisors are promoted into their first supervisory position from a nonsupervisory job within the same organization. Teaching people how to treat you involves carrying yourself in a professional manner and using sensitive interpersonal skills.

Overcoming your prior image may be a challenge, but it is possible. Guided reflection is the foundation of learning. We must learn from our past experiences and use what we learn to become more effective in the future.

The temptation to please management by increasing productivity may cause you to be less sensitive to the people in your department and their problems. This insensitivity is a serious mistake. Support from others you trust can help you deal effectively with change. Involve your team members in planning, decision making, and problem solving. Some of your team members may know more about your department than you do.

DISCUSSION QUESTIONS

1. In moving from the position of team member to hospitality supervisor, what basic behavioral changes should you anticipate?

2. In making the transition to supervisor in the same company, how would you go about building a supervisor–team member relationship with a team member you were close friends with before the switch?

3. If you were the director of human resources, how would you communicate with and try to change the attitude of a new supervisor who had become overly impressed with the power of his or her new position?

4. How would you balance home life and work life so that one does not jeopardize the other?

5. What typical mistakes should a new supervisor try to avoid making?

PART II

CREATING A SUCCESSFUL TEAM

Your main duties as a supervisor are to manage people and ensure your team's productivity. To do this you need strong interpersonal skills: You must know how to motivate people and build relationships, and you need to know how to provide your team with an environment conducive to productivity. In this part we talk about these needs and how to fulfill them in your operation.

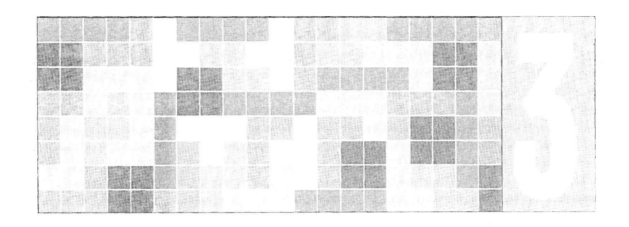

Working With and Developing Your Team

You wear many hats as a hospitality supervisor. One of the hospitality supervisor's primary goals is to help others excel. This means that you will spend your time observing and responding to the performance exhibited by your team members. You will need to set performance goals, develop training, and find ways to improve your operations. Too many supervisors in the hospitality industry spend their time doing the work of their team instead of empowering their team members and holding them accountable for their own work. When this happens employees end up supplementing the efforts of supervisors who have convinced themselves that they are responsible for carrying the workload of the operation.

Question: *How long will team members allow you to do their work?*

Answer: *For as long as you are willing and able to do it.*

After you have finished reading this chapter, you should be able to

- explain your role in developing your team members,

- discuss how to evaluate and communicate standards of performance,

- identify the characteristics of a critic and an evaluator, and

- explain why it is important to model the behavior you desire from team members.

SUPERVISOR AS LEADER

Your job as the leader means modeling the behavior that others should emulate. It means adjusting your leadership behavior to accommodate their needs. There will be times when your team will need you to lead the way and be involved directly with the operations. There will be other times when you can supervise the activities of the operations without directly doing the work and relying solely on the efforts of your team. There also will be times when your role is to think about and plan for future challenges and events.

Supervisor as Leader to Self

Focus on managing your personal life better now so that you can handle more responsibility, such as leading a department, later. Don't perform tasks that don't require your level of expertise. Ask yourself, "Would I pay another supervisor to do this task"? By focusing on managing yourself you learn to

- concentrate on what's really important,

- establish goals,

- set priorities,

- manage your time, and

- make good decisions.

Don't allow self-imposed limitations prevent you from excelling in your job. You are limited by your knowledge, and you are responsible for your own development. Other people, including your boss, should help you, but it is your responsibility to seek out and create opportunities to gain new knowledge and experiences. Be a continuous student.

- Take classes. Outside training will give you a fresh perspective on assessing daily activities on the job.

- Subscribe to industry publications to stay abreast of current events in the industry. Attend industry conferences and workshops as well.

- Identify your own strengths and weaknesses. Don't wait until someone tells you to learn a new skill or subject matter. Take the initiative to learn new things yourself.

- Find a mentor. Take advantage of peers' expertise to broaden your own skills.

Supervisor as Company Leader

You have an obligation to your company to represent yourself in a manner that reflects positively on the company. Your behavior and decisions must be legally, morally, ethically, and logically driven. As a company representative, you symbolize the values and essence of the operation; the repercussions of your behavior and decisions cast an effect far beyond you and can include every shareholder and stakeholder in the company.

SUPERVISOR AS DEVELOPER

Your job is to acknowledge and respond to performance—good or bad. In your role as a developer, your mission is to increase the skills and knowledge of your team members. To do this you must have the right frame of mind. You already know that the people you supervise work for you. What you may not know is that you work for them. They determine your success; they can help you gain your next promotion. They can also send you packing.

Your job also requires that you contribute to the success of your organization and to those you lead. You do this by creating ways to advance their knowledge and skills.

Model the Behavior You Want from Your Team Members

Too many hospitality leaders fail to match their actions to their words. Hospitably leaders influence their team by what they say and do. For example, as a supervisor, if you tell a team member to wash his hands, he washes his hands. Why? Team members do what you tell them because they recognize your position, your authority, and your credibility. What you say matters to your team members.

What you do matters to your team members as well. You may constantly tell team members to wash their hands before and after prepping chicken. Team members learn what is right based on what you say, but team members are always watching you. They know what you eat, how long you are on break, and how hard you are working. If you are prepping chicken and you fail to wash your hands, who saw you? Your team members. This action speaks as loud as (if not louder than) words.

You are a model to your team members. They listen and watch, so consistently model the behavior you expect from your team members.

The *Harvard Business Review* (September 2002) published a study that depicted the impact of managers who failed to "do what they say." A total of 6500 team members at 76 U.S. and Canadian hotels were studied. Using a five-point scale, they were asked to rank how well their leaders' behaviors, words, and actions were aligned. Team members ranked their managers using various statements regarding their supervisors' behavior in the workplace. Example responses included the following:

■ "My manager delivers on promises."

■ "My manager practices what she preaches."

Team members also were asked to rank their supervisors' commitment and the service environment of their establishment on a five-point scale. Example responses included

■ "I am proud to tell others I am part of this hotel."

■ "My co-workers go out of their way to accommodate guests' special requests."

Survey results were correlated and linked to the hotels' customer satisfaction surveys, personnel records, and financial records. These study results showed that the hotels in which team members strongly believed their leaders delivered on promises and practiced what they preached ("walked the talk") were more profitable than hotels where team members ranked their leaders at average or below average for matching their behavior with their words. Furthermore, it was found that managers who scored high on the five-point scale could be expected to increase their hotel's profitability by 2.5% of revenues. "In this study, that translates to a profit increase of more than $250,000.00 per year per hotel. *No other single aspect* of manager behavior that was measured by the study had as large an impact on profits."[1]

Recognizing and Responding to Performance

Modeling behavior you want employees to exhibit can go a long way toward affecting performance, but there are other ways to recognize and respond to operational and individual performance. One of the most important things you'll do as a hospitality supervisor is improve your team's performance, as the Harvard study showed. To improve this performance, you must first observe it, evaluate it, and respond.

[1]*Harvard Business Review*, September 2002, #103.

Operational Performance

A goal to keep in mind when observing performance is to analyze problem areas of your operations and to work with your team members to resolve problems. These types of problems are less of an individual performance issue and more of an operational issue. Look for the bottlenecks—particularly during the busy periods of the day. What areas of operations appear to be suffering? In the restaurant environment the bottleneck often occurs throughout the meal period. For example, in a cafeteria-style restaurant bottlenecks can occur at the following points:

- When receiving your guests. If you are not adequately staffed or the structure of your establishment is restricted, you may not be able to move your customers in an orderly and timely manner.

- When ordering. Customers are entitled to have time to make choices about their meal selection. The more complicated your menu is, the longer they need to make a decision.

- During meal preparations. Although many food items are premade, special requests and plate presentations add time to customers' overall experience.

- At the time of payment. The payment process can create bottlenecks as customers look for change or wait for credit card approvals.

- During service. Servers in the dining room must be on their toes to maximize the opportunities to give quality service and to turn tables. If the wait staff is slow or making mistakes, the potential for bottleneck problems increases.

- In bussing and dishroom tasks. Waiting on clean silverware and dishware can easily become a source of frustration for you and your customers if this aspect of your operations is not properly staffed and efficient. The productivity and thoroughness of the dishroom affects every customer and team member.

Individual Performance

Your evaluation of and response to your team's performance should be an ongoing process. Don't limit your comments to the annual review process; give your staff feedback every day. The following performance evaluation tree shows the process of establishing and communicating standards of performance.

Evaluating Performance.   The purpose of evaluating performance is to recognize the performer. If the performance meets expectations, you should praise the performer because praising the person encourages the performance to be repeated.

When the performance is wrong, you will either have to train or discipline the performer. Training allows you the opportunity to educate the person to perform to expectations. Discipline addresses performance that fails to meet expectations.

Reevaluating Performance.   The purpose of reevaluating performance is to recognize the performer and document changes in performance.

Evaluating Performance Model

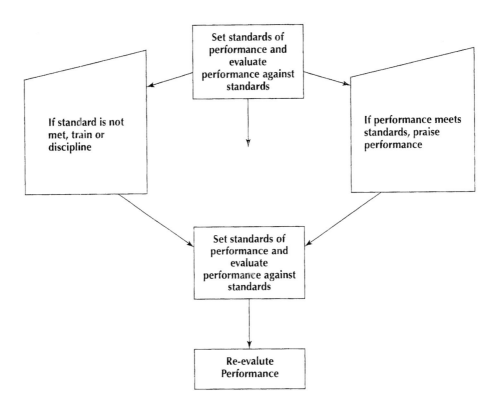

Evaluator or Critic

Unfortunately, most team members expect and most supervisors deliver the wrong response when evaluating performance. Most team members view managers as critics; there is a difference between being an evaluator and a critic.

A critic is a person who passes judgment on performance. This is a person who tends to

- demoralize the value of the individual,

- fail to recognize what is right in performance,

- find fault in the person performing the job,

- focus more on being understood rather than understanding,

- identify rather than address the problem,

- be perceived in a negative light by team members,

- take action to correct the problem today but fail to implement a permanent solution, and

- be hard on the person rather than the problem.

A CRITIC'S TALE

Anthony is a hard worker who is willing to learn. He has been training as a night auditor and front desk attendant for two weeks. He works the third shift and his supervisor lives onsite. Tonight is his first night going solo, and the hotel expects to be sold out.

At 11:00 P.M., while checking in a family of four with a one-year-old with a sour stomach, a bus arrives full of people checking into the hotel. As the lobby begins to fill, another couple returns to the front desk complaining that their room is dirty and demanding to be moved to another room or refunded their money.

While completing the check-in for the family of four, the computer crashes. Anthony can't assign rooms, issue keys, or issue refunds. After numerous attempts to reset the computer, Anthony realizes he is in trouble. He calls his supervisor, who tells him to reboot the system. Anthony reboots the system and it fails.

The one-year-old starts to cry. The family of four becomes irritated. The lobby crowd grows impatient, and the couple with the dirty room becomes angrier. Anthony calls his supervisor, who tells him to reboot the system. Anthony reboots the system and it fails.

It is now after midnight. Anthony calls his supervisor again. His supervisor, Ted, angrily storms into the lobby and openly questions Anthony's ability to do his job. Ted apologizes to the crowd for Anthony's shortcomings and he tells them he will take care of them as quickly as possible. Ted reboots the system and it works. Ted glares at Anthony and tells him to do his job as he walks away from the front desk to return to his room.

Anthony begins checking in the family of four. The computer crashes. He calls his supervisor again. As Ted approaches the front desk, he angrily questions Anthony's ability to do his job. Ted reboots the system. When he turns to address Anthony again, he finds that Anthony is gone.

Ted ends up working the remainder of Anthony's shift.

An evaluator, on the other hand, is a person who appraises performance. This person tends to

- find strengths of the person performing the job,

- focus more on understanding rather than being understood,

- identify and teach ways to improve performance,

- increase the value of the individual,

- be perceived in a positive light by team members,

- recognize what is right in performance,

- take action to improve performance by implementing and teaching permanent solutions, and

- be easy on the person and hard on the problem.

Helping Others Perform Better through Recognition

Everyone deserves to be recognized and rewarded for his or her work. Recognition is a prime motivator for successful performers. A "pat on the back" from one's supervisor in recognition for a job well done helps build strong and lasting relationships.

Recognition given by fellow teammates is also extremely rewarding. Supervisors should encourage their team members to give each other recognition when deserved. Well-deserved recognition from peers and supervisors strengthens relationships, which enhances productivity and morale.

All supervisors should understand the importance of recognizing the performance of their team, but too many managers in the hospitality industry have credit problems. We are not talking about the credit problems associated with financial well-being. The credit problems we are referring to pertain to recognition. Too many managers are so focused on acquiring recognition for themselves that they neglect to give their team members the recognition they deserve.

It is dangerous to be a self-centered leader when your success largely depends on the performance of your team members. Being self-centered and helping other people are conflicting priorities. As a leader responsible for the performance of other people, you cannot afford to be self-centered. Team members have a knack for knowing when their boss takes all the credit for their work. Self-centered managers can become so absorbed in seeking the recognition spotlight that they often steal the praise belonging to someone else. They inflate their contributions to group projects and overstate the significance of their role. Self-centered managers completely fail to understand the link between recognition of their team and the increased value of their worth to their company.

Supervisors who focus on securing recognition for themselves fail to elevate, support, or seek recognition for their team. When this happens, team members will reduce their efforts to perform to their capability because they do not feel their efforts will be recognized or rewarded. If this continues, productivity will decline and the supervisor's effectiveness will be questioned.

Supervisors who focus on elevating, supporting, and seeking recognition for the members of their staff will find that staff members will repeat performance that is recognized or rewarded and the supervisor will gain recognition because of the performance of his or her staff.

CONCLUSION

Too many supervisors in the hospitality industry spend their time doing the work of their team instead of empowering their team members and holding them accountable for their own work. Don't perform tasks that don't require your level of expertise. Ask yourself, "Would I pay another supervisor to do this task"? Your behavior and decisions must be legally, morally, ethically, and logically driven. Your evaluation of and response to your team's performance should be an ongoing process. Don't limit your comments to the annual review process; give your staff feedback every day. According to research, recognition continues to be the number one motivation for successful performers. A "pat on the back" from one's supervisor in recognition for a job well done helps build strong and lasting relationships.

DISCUSSION QUESTIONS

1. Describe the opportunities that were missed by the supervisor in "A Critic's Tale." Explain how you would have handled the same situation.

2. How does a manager's ability to do what she says affect the financials of an establishment? How does it affect the morale of the team members?

3. How would an evaluator resolve the same situation discussed in "A Critic's Tale"?

4. Why is it important to improve your team's performance? How would you do this?

5. What are some types of training you could develop to help your team improve its performance?

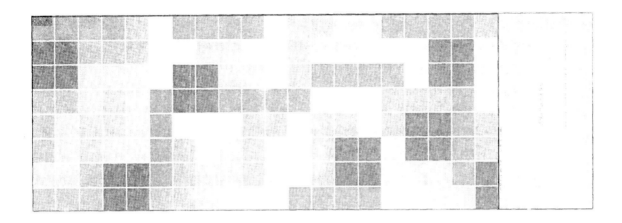

People: Your Key to Productivity and Profit

It is *good* that you know and can do what needs to be done.
It will be *great* when your team can perform as well as you do.

After you have finished reading this chapter, you should be able to

■ list three reasons why a supervisor must work with people to gain productivity,

■ list the five principles for effective human relations,

■ explain the productivity formula,

■ explain the three characteristics of a motivating environment, and

■ explain how to achieve higher productivity through total quality relationships.

ACHIEVING PRODUCTIVITY THROUGH PEOPLE

As you transition from the role of worker to that of supervisor, you will experience many transformations. Your vision will change; instead of focusing solely on your job performance, you will begin to see how everyone's contributions affect the overall operation. You will understand the link among people, performance, and profit. People are the key piece in this equation, and you must learn to appreciate and value the people on your team. Remember, people get better when the supervisor gets better.

Your attention will shift from things to people, from the job itself to the person who performs the job. In short, you will become people oriented. You suddenly will find yourself more interested in John than in the dishwasher he operates and more concerned with Helen than with the entrees she cooks.

Terms such as *human relations, human behavior, motivation, attitude, sensitivity,* and *leadership style* will take on new meaning. Human understanding will earn the same priority as job know-how. Helping Roberta increase her productivity will be as important as writing schedules within labor guidelines, and improving Dick's attitude will command your attention along with customer service, food safety, and sanitation. You must make the shift from a job-centered team member to a people-centered supervisor.

Why is this transition necessary? Why must a supervisor learn to focus attention more on people than on the job itself? The answer lies in a simple, basic truth: A supervisor achieves productivity through people. Your success will be determined by the output of those you supervise.

Your individual productivity, no matter how hard or long you work, will *never* match the productivity of your team. As a supervisor, you are responsible for the productivity of everyone in your department. Consequently, management will be interested in measuring departmental productivity and not what you produce yourself.

Obviously, you cannot increase productivity substantially through your own production. You cannot supervise effectively and produce at a high level at the same time—you are only one person, not two or three. Even if you arrive at work two hours early and leave two hours late every day to do production work, the increase in total productivity would not be substantial, and, of course, you could not continue at such a pace for long.

The moment you become a supervisor, the production work you do yourself becomes secondary to the relationships you build with the people who do most of the actual work. Even though you may be able to do the job better or faster than those who work for you, and even though you would enjoy doing it yourself, you must turn it over to your team members. You must achieve desired productivity levels by learning how to direct, train, create, and maintain a motivating environment.

When you become a supervisor, you must learn to let the personal satisfaction of working with people replace the satisfaction you previously gained by working with things. Your future is in the hands of those you supervise, so you must take pride in creating the kinds of relationships that will motivate people to achieve the productivity you desire. First, create the relationships, and then work through them to achieve your productivity goals.

To do this you must create and maintain an atmosphere of respect and trust. By listening and following through on your team members' suggestions, going to bat for them with your superiors, recognizing their individuality, and, above all, demonstrating two-way communication, you will build trusting relationships with your team members.

THE PRODUCTIVITY FORMULA

Productivity is a word dear to the hearts of all organizations. In its broadest meaning, productivity is the major pursuit of all American business and government organizations, and it forms the foundation of our profit system. It permits us to compete favorably within our industry.

Simply put, productivity equals *output divided by input*. It is written as the formula

$$P \text{ (productivity)} = \frac{O \text{ (output)}}{I \text{ (input)}}$$

By manipulating output or input we affect productivity. In hospitality, high productivity usually means that the organization is efficient in providing its services to its customers.

The more efficient the operation the more successful it will be.

Output is anything your company produces. Inputs are the things it takes to produce output. For example, one person in a delicatessen produces 100 of the deli's signature sandwiches in 2 hours. Productivity for making those sandwiches is calculated by plugging this data into the productivity formula:

$$\text{Sandwich productivity} = \frac{\text{Output (100 sandwiches)}}{\text{Input (2 hours)}}$$

Dividing 100 by 2 hours provides the productivity for making the sandwiches. In this case, this individual's productivity in making these sandwiches is

50 sandwiches per hour of work

The rate of productivity affects the unit cost for producing the sandwiches. If our sandwich maker collects $8.00 per hour worked and it takes him 1 hour to make 50 sandwiches, the cost per sandwich is calculated by dividing $8.00 by 50 sandwiches. The result gives us the amount of money it costs—in labor to make one sandwich.

$$\frac{\$8.00 \text{ (labor cost)}}{50 \text{ sandwiches}} = \$.16 \text{ or } 16 \text{ cents}$$

It takes 16 cents to produce each sandwich. Knowing the level of productivity can help the organization establish the correct price to charge its customers for its goods or services.

There are many ways to increase productivity. Reducing mistakes, errors, and waste of any kind; training employees; and investing in modern and efficient equipment are a few common ways to increase productivity. In some form or another all organizations measure their productivity. Productivity levels can be calculated on a single operation or task. It can also be calculated on the organization as a whole. The organization's level of productivity provides evidence on its overall efficiency and financial health. Supervisors who raise productivity without sacrificing the expected level of quality add value to their organization. Adding value is a sure way to success.

PRODUCTIVITY IN THE HOSPITALITY INDUSTRY

In the hospitality industry, it is too often assumed that being busy is the same as being productive. Being productive means the accomplishment of activities that support the attainment of departmental goals. Engaging in activities that do not support the goals of the department is counterproductive and wasteful. Being productive means doing the right things at the right time. It is managing your "controllables." Ultimately, productivity is measured in sales, customer count, and profits.

Sales: The flow of money into your operation from "paying" customers

Customer Count: The actual number of people visiting your establishment

Profit: The amount of money left over after all expenses are paid

Sales

Money flowing into your operation is critical to your success. If money is not flowing through your doors, you fail—period. It doesn't matter how nice you are, or how wonderfully creative you may be, or how much your team members like you, or how many hours you work. If you are not building sales, your company is going to replace you.

As callous as it sounds, in the end, it's all business. Companies are in business to make money, and you have been hired to achieve this goal.

However, if you are not nice, creative, and hard working, and if your team members don't like you, you will *never*, we repeat, NEVER, grow your sales. Customers get what team members get. Remember this: If you treat your team members badly, they will share their experience with your customers. Sales are not built on bad service. You have to focus on taking care of the people who are closest to the customers if you want to have any hopes of building your sales.

Your company (or you, if you are the owner) will need to engage in various marketing activities to grow sales. Since our focus is management, we will not discuss the various things you can do to grow sales in this book. However, there are three critical points you need to understand about sales:

1. No matter what marketing strategy you engage in, it will never be successful if your operation isn't right. Think of it this way, you should never invite anyone to your house unless your house is in order.

2. Paying customers build sales. Nonpaying customers may grow business for future revenue, and you will need this type of customer for various reasons. Until they pay, nonpaying customers are an operating expense, sometimes call an opportunity cost.

   > John pays for his hotel room using his credit card. Susan's room was complimentary. The hotel manager wanted her to spend the evening in hopes she would book her fifty-person family reunion with them. Housekeeping has to clean both their rooms. Only John is paying for the service.

3. Often, organizations engage in complimentary offers to boost future sales. It's an old adage that you have to spend money to make money. Controllables like labor, food, training, inventory, preventive maintenance, and free offers may increase costs in the short run. They may have significant benefits in the long term, however. The more profits you generate in sales, the easier it is to justify spending some of your budget on opportunity costs.

Customer Count

No matter what your business is, customers are vital to it. The more customers you have, the more successful your business will be. If you are not retaining regular customers and attracting new customers, you will not be in business long.

Some companies camouflage how well they are doing with their customers by playing with numbers. When customer count is down, they often increase their price to show an increase in sales. They are bringing in more money but not more customers. If your prices are raised and your customers do not perceive an increase in value to them, they are going to leave you. Companies that raise their price without increasing their offering to their customers are subjecting their customers to price abuse. What they are doing is making the customers pay more for the service they are getting. At some point, this ploy yields a negative result. Customers will only endure so much price abuse before they move elsewhere. Customers will not allow themselves to be taken advantage of forever. The number of regular customers you retain and the number of new customers you attract are keys to success.

Profit

The purpose of your organization is to make money. If you increase your sales and your customer counts but mismanage your budget, you are not doing your job. The difference between what you spend and what you deposit at the bank is your profit.

CATEGORIES OF PRODUCTIVITY

There are two categories of productivity that supervisors need to know about: individual and departmental productivity.

Individual Productivity

As the term implies, individual productivity is the performance or contribution of one person over a specified period of time. It may refer to the number of customers served, the amount of food prepared, the number of new products developed, the sales achieved, or the quality of customer service rendered by an individual.

> At 7:00 A.M. the breakfast line was out the door. Dwight watched Richard kick into high gear and seemingly do the impossible. Like a whirlwind, he single-handedly cooked every order without flaw, scrambling, grilling, slicing, and dicing with perfection. Dwight marveled at how one person could accomplish so much.

The productivity of all individuals is measured to some extent. If an objective measurement is impossible, a subjective measurement is attempted, perhaps by comparing one individual with another. The measurement of individuals is vital to good personnel administration. The important thing, of course, is to measure the productivity and not the personality of the individual.

Departmental Productivity

Departmental productivity is the sum total of all productivity that comes from a department or section within an organization. Like individual productivity it also can be tangible; it can be measured in sales, customer service, or a combination of these. Just as one individual is compared with another, a department's contribution to the operation is compared to other departments.

It is easier, however, to measure the productivity of a department with more objective data because it usually can be reduced to figures and accounting information. It's important to realize that departmental productivity becomes your responsibility the moment you become a supervisor. You must live with the figures, reports, and comparisons on a day-to-day basis. How are your sales this year compared to the same time last year? How are your sales compared to other units within the company? If productivity goes up, you are rewarded; if it goes down, you must come up with some explanations. Your reputation in the company will be tied to the productivity record of your department regardless of how much you contribute individually.

A supervisor's goal is to improve departmental productivity. Because supervisors have a limited supply of time and energy, their time and energy should be spent helping team members improve individual productivity; this, in turn, will improve overall productivity. This goal is accomplished primarily by building better human relationships with team members and creating an environment in which they will be motivated to reach their own potential.

Take a look at the following examples of how different supervisors handled achieving this goal.

1. Despite the fact that Woody felt he already had more than he could handle, he was given new duties in the bakery in addition to his responsibilities running the back of the house (BOH) kitchen operations, where he had been a supervisor for five years. How could he pitch in during high-activity periods in the kitchen operations if he had to supervise workers in the bakery? He decided to lay his cards on the table with his 12-person kitchen operations staff. His comment was, "In the past I've been able to help out during peak periods, but I can no longer do it. In the future it will be up to you to maintain productivity without my personal productivity unless there is an emergency. How you do this is up to you. If you can come up with some time-saving procedures, I will go along with them."

   Six weeks later, after the crew had made a number of helpful suggestions, food production during the meal period were achieved without personal help from Woody, and when one member of the staff resigned, a replacement was not necessary. Woody learned that his crew had not been working up to their potential because they could rely on him to step in and produce during busy periods.

2. Alice, a housekeeping manager for a major hotel chain, devoted so much time to training new people to prepare guest rooms that other team members felt neglected. She finally turned guest room training over to another team member. Because she was able to improve relationships by making this change, efficiency increased to the point where the facility was able to maintain a higher level of customer satisfaction.

3. Frieda, general manager of a school cafeteria, decided to delegate a series of duties to her assistant managers so that she could devote more time to building relationships with the students (her customers). By spending more time with the students, she was able to develop more appealing menu items, and this led to an increase in sales.

The new supervisor soon learns that a difference almost always exists between a team member's daily performance and his or her capacity to perform. Whether large or small, a productivity gap of some size is natural and should be expected in all team members. Such gaps are, of course, difficult to measure accurately for two reasons:

1. The true potential capacity of an individual cannot really be determined because it is made up of several elusive factors, such as mental ability, inner drive, perception, attitude, physical stamina, and emotional stability.

2. Job productivity is difficult to measure. The actual performance of a worker is fluid, moving up and down on an hourly, daily, and weekly basis (anybody can have an off day). Productivity levels quickly move up and down depending on many internal and environmental factors. The supervisor can control some, but not all, of these factors.

It is only natural that supervisors should be sensitive to changes in productivity levels in their team members. When a team member shows progress in closing the gap between the current level of productivity and the potential capacity, the supervisor is happy. When the opposite happens, the supervisor becomes disturbed. The smaller the gap, the greater the total productivity, and nothing is more important to the supervisor's personal success.

MOTIVATION THEORIES

How do supervisors motivate their employees to work more productively? How can productivity be increase without hiring more team members? Management books are full of motivational theories. Some, properly interpreted, can be useful to the beginning supervisor. We will examine some sound principles for creating and maintaining motivating environments.

Hawthorne Experiments

From 1927 to 1932, the Western Electric Company conducted what are now known as the Hawthorne experiments.[1] These experiments showed that no matter what kind of improvements were made (e.g., improved lighting, breaks, free hot lunches), the productivity of the work group increased. Even when those things like breaks were taken away, productivity still rose. Why? One conclusion was that the team members' productivity was related to human relation factors. The experimental work group felt that their supervisors valued them as people. The supportive attention provided by supervisors to their workers during the experiment affected productivity more than any change to the work environment. Until these experiments were made, management had accepted that the way to improve the rate of production was to improve machinery, provide better lighting, and make similar physical changes. The Hawthorne experiments proved that the attention paid to workers affects motivation and productivity in a positive way.

Motivation Is Internal

The ideal working climate is one that creates self-motivation in workers. It is generally recognized today that in most work environments traditional motivational techniques do not work well. Supervisors get little response from most workers through pep talks, contests, or small pay increases. In a large number of cases, a worker is either self-motivated or not motivated at all. The word *motivation* comes from Latin and means literally, "to move." Machinery cannot move on its own. For example, for a clock to move it needs some motivating force, some energy source external to itself, like a wound main spring, battery, or other source of energy. On the other hand, movement or motivation is internal to living organisms. For example, we cannot motivate or force an orange to grow; it either grows or it doesn't. If we want to grow an orange we plant an

[1] Elton Mayo, *The Human Problem*, 1934.

orange seed and create and maintain the right kind of conditions, including the best soil, sunlight, moisture, and temperature. Once the seed is planted, we must wait for it to germinate. No amount of coaxing will motivate it to grow. Maintaining the proper environment may enhance the possibility that the orange seed will be motivated to grow but does not guarantee that the orange seed will grow into a tree and bear fruit. As living organisms, our employees are not machines, and their motivation is internal to them. Like the orange, the person chooses to move.

The supervisor is challenged to create an environment where, without prodding, employees will want to achieve. In short, employees "catch" motivation from the surrounding climate, a climate created primarily by the way the supervisor supervises. When an atmosphere of confidence and involvement is created, the employee feels good about his or her role and wants to reach out to achieve. Creating and holding on to such a climate is one of the most difficult challenges both new and experienced supervisors face.

Three Characteristics of Motivating Environments

Research has shown that environments conducive to internal motivation share the following three characteristics. They provide

1. Purposeful and meaningful work for employees

2. Continuous learning

3. Accurate, timely, and specific feedback on performance

Let us look closely at each of these characteristics.

Purposeful and Meaningful Work

Supervisors must communicate to their employees that they consider them to be valuable to the company. Saying it to them is necessary but not sufficient. Here are some things that supervisors can do to create purposeful and meaningful work for their employees:

1. Involve them in planning changes. Many times employees are only informed or included in the change process at the implementation stage. When possible, include your employees in change from the beginning: involve them in the planning stage of a change.

2. Meet with employees as a group on a regular basis. During the meeting, dedicate a portion of time to seek their input and opinions on issues important to the department, not only when planning change but in solving problems and making decisions. This is especially important when the solution of a problem changes any aspect of an employee's work routine.

3. Show them how their contribution affects their department's welfare or that of the company's. In some cases the supervisor may be able to show how the company's products or services enhance the lives of its customers and society in general.

Sometimes employees are told that if they don't like what is happening they can quit. Do not send such a message unless you are prepared to deal with a negative reaction. Doing or saying things that devalue employee contributions like this quickly and thoroughly undermine the feeling of having purposeful and meaningful work.

Continuous Learning

A job that continually challenges the employee to learn is crucial to motivation. If a job is mastered easily, it may become boring or monotonous to the one doing it. Motivating environments contain elements that require the employee to build new skills in order to complete the job. Here are some things the supervisor can do:

- Engage in continuous improvement. Encourage your employees to seek new techniques, new technology, or improvements to the existing work.

- Provide opportunities for employees to learn more about their job, company, or industry. Many companies provide in-service training on a variety of topics, like new computer software, financial planning, or supervision. The supervisor can set the example by personally engaging in training opportunities.

Employees can really get hooked on training and development at work. A well-trained employee who seeks to keep his or her skills current is a motivated employee.

Accurate, Timely, and Specific Feedback on Performance

Employees want to know how well they are performing. Feedback is the cornerstone of growth as well as for productivity. Many companies formally evaluate employee performance at specific times. Annual or semiannual evaluations are the norm. Probationary employees are often evaluated more often during their probationary period. Performance appraisals affect employees in very important ways. The outcomes of the performance appraisal often affect pay raises, job security, promotions, and other important employment decisions. All of these are extremely important to the employee. Supervisors doing appraisals should keep the following in mind:

1. Do the appraisal on or before the due date. The longer the appraisal is put off, the less effective it will be.

2. Take time to cover the results of the appraisal with the employee. The appraisal conference should be done in private and each area appraised should be discussed thoroughly.

3. Allow your employees receiving the appraisal to ask questions for clarification.

4. If the performance appraisal procedure allows, let your employees appraise their own performance and have them bring their appraisal to the conference. The supervisor also completes an appraisal and, during the conference, compares and contrasts the contents of the appraisal form both perspectives. Sometimes a self-appraisal reveals pertinent information.

5. Provide a blank appraisal form to the employee at the beginning of the appraisal period. Encourage the employee to study its contents and, as time goes by, discuss any ambiguities or questions that the employee may have regarding what behavior is being assed and how that behavior is rated. Employees should not be surprised or blindsided by the results of their appraisal.

The extent that supervisors provide employees with these things will determine employees' level of self-motivation. The higher the self-motivation, the more employees will work in helping their supervisor and organization meet stated goals.

SEVEN WAYS TO INCREASE PRODUCTIVITY

During the last few decades, the hospitality industry has become competitive for the attention and patronage of paying customers. Businesses recognize that productivity can improve with accountability.

The hospitality industry is a robust environment of constant change resulting from the almost never-ending demands to improve core competencies in services and products. Flawed by high turnover rates in the labor pool, the industry is in a constant battle to improve the productivity of its employees. To achieve greater employee productivity, keep these seven important principles in mind:

1. Building good relations with team members is more important than being able to do the job skillfully yourself. The technical skills you have are important because you must know how to do something before you can teach and supervise others; however, your emphasis as a supervisor will be on transmitting your skills rather than doing the tasks yourself.

   Your future promotions will be based on the productivity of the people who work for you now. Many factors are considered when management promotes a first-line supervisor to a more responsible middle management position, but nothing influences a favorable decision more than a supervisor's having the human relations skills to motivate sustained productivity from people. To ignore, underestimate, or downgrade this principle in any way will surely damage your career.

2. Spending time to restore or improve your relationship with a team member whose productivity has slipped is one of the most important things you can do with your time.

   As a supervisor, you will have multiple responsibilities. In all likelihood, you will have more things to do than time to do them, so it will be necessary to sift out and assign suitable priorities to your responsibilities. Top priority should always go to keeping the productivity of others as high as possible. When the productivity of one team member slips, you must be aware of it immediately and begin trying to do something about it within a reasonable period of time.

3. Management expects you to achieve high productivity from new team members in a hurry. Today faster payoff is expected from new team members for

several reasons: (a) The supervisor may be faced with high turnover rates. (b) The pace in most organizations is fast. Orientation periods have been sped up, and training time (both on the job and in formal classrooms) is more limited. (c) Training is expensive.

What do these factors mean to you as a supervisor? It means you must build relations with new team members as early as possible and train them quickly so that they reach a good productivity level in a shorter span of time.

4. When you think of higher productivity, you must think of quality. Corporations have discovered that higher productivity and higher quality are necessary to compete domestically and internationally. Stockholders and executives know they are dependent on front-line supervisors to achieve these goals.

5. Productivity is performance that is observed and measured. A mistake novice and even experienced managers make is assessing performance arbitrarily and subjectively.

6. If not already completed, a job analysis must be conducted to determine the function of every position. This analysis should define the behavioral objectives that the team member will need to perform.

7. If you want to invoke a change in productivity of your team members, you must take the attitude that if you have not told them what you want, and if you have not shown them what you want, they don't know what you want.

TOTAL QUALITY RELATIONSHIPS

Creating and maintaining a motivational environment is possible for the supervisor who values his or her people. Achieving total quality relationships (TQRs) with your employees is as possible and important as having total quality products and services. To achieve total quality relationships with your employees, remember to provide the following five principles for TQR.

Five Principles of TQR:

1. Give clear and complete instructions.

2. Communicate: Let your people know how they are doing and provide counseling when necessary.

3. Give credit when it is due.

4. Involve people in decisions.

5. Maintain an open door policy.

These simple, somewhat obvious, fundamentals really work and are recognized as irreplaceable by expert supervisors. They are easy to understand, psychologically healthy, and have passed the test of time.

Principle 1: Give Clear and Complete Instructions

As a supervisor, you have a certain amount of "knowledge power." You know more about how to perform certain tasks than most of your team members. How effectively you transmit this knowledge to them is the key to the relationship created.

When instructions are given clearly and completely, team members know exactly what to do and they feel good about it; however, when the instructions are hazy and incomplete, team members lose confidence in the supervisor, and the relationship between them deteriorates. To feel secure, team members must know what is expected and be given the opportunity to build the skills to do their jobs. This kind of help mainly comes from the supervisor.

Make sure to take time in giving instructions. When possible, use visual illustrations and follow the basic teaching techniques of keeping things simple and logical and providing examples. In addition, ask for feedback from the team members at the time the instructions are given and follow-up by checking the following day to see whether the instructions were put into practice correctly.

> With many important problems facing him, Jake took time to demonstrate patiently to Mary, an insecure new team member, how to operate a complicated, dangerous machine. Jake gave Mary more than two hours of his time, including two follow-ups, so that all errors were eliminated. On her second day at work, Mary felt completely competent and her productivity was almost up to average. This training happened more than a year ago, and Mary has yet to have an accident. Furthermore, Jake has had a strong, sound relationship with Mary from the very start.

Principle 2: Communicate: Let Your People Know How They Are Doing and Provide Counseling When Necessary

To keep supervisor–team member relationships in good repair, take time to let team members know how they are getting along. Let them know whether they are doing well or not. Most team members (especially new ones) want to know how to do their jobs better and will welcome help if it is provided in a constructive way. They also want to know when things are going well and when you are pleased with their performance. Don't let them feel that they are working in a vacuum.

The thing that hurts team members most is neglect. They want to feel that they are an important part of the department, and they know that their future depends on your training and support. An excellent way to keep the relationship in good working order is to provide both training and support. Being open to the needs of your team members will help create effective two-way communication.

> Mrs. Browne is a highly capable night supervisor of housekeepers in an Atlanta hospital. She does not, however, believe in letting people know how well they are doing. She almost never tells a housekeeper when she or he does well, but she

comes down heavily when a violation occurs. As a result, she has more personnel problems than any supervisor on the staff. Housekeepers are constantly asking to be transferred to other wards. Mrs. Browne has been passed over for a promotion for three years in succession.

Principle 3: Give Credit When it is Due

Team members need positive reinforcement if they are to keep their personal productivity at a high level. They need the compliment you intend to give before you get too busy with something else; they need recognition. Sometimes it is best to give credit in front of the entire department. More often, however, it is best given privately. Praise should be given freely, sincerely, and, most important, when it is due. To achieve this goal, you must constantly have your "radar" turned on to observe behavior that is deserving of credit. Supervisors who fail to give credit when it is due often have standards that are far above levels the team members are capable of reaching. This attitude leaves team members feeling small and insignificant and usually results in lower productivity. It is necessary to be sincere in giving credit, and it is wise to be generous with giving it.

> Karen handles deposits for her company's 200 restaurant units, which have accumulated large sums of deposits. Many managers often fail to transmit their deposit information to the home office on time, creating cash flow disparities. Last week at a staff meeting, Karen's supervisor complimented the entire staff on the improvements they had made in getting managers to transit their deposits on time and singled out Karen for special mention. The following day Karen told her supervisor that she appreciated the pat on the back and thanked the supervisor.

Principle 4: Involve Your Employees in Decisions

Certain problems may arise that only the supervisor can solve. The wise supervisor knows, however, that many problems can be solved with team member participation. When you involve team members in departmental problems that concern them, you accomplish three goals:

1. You give them a chance to learn about the operations of the department, thus preparing them for future promotions.

2. You build their confidence by providing decision-making opportunities, and, as a result, their productivity increases.

3. You improve the departmental climate by bringing people closer together and reduce friction and misunderstandings.

Often the secondary benefits of letting team members come up with solutions to problems are more helpful than the solutions themselves. When team members help make decisions, they grow and you gain. Involvement makes people feel important, challenged, and stimulated. It can release talent and increase productivity as nothing else can.

Make it a practice to turn over appropriate problems to the people who work for you. Let them struggle with solutions even if you could easily find the answer alone. Once they have an answer, accept it gracefully, giving their solution your full support. Team members often give greater support to their decisions than to those handed down by the supervisor. Do not, however, come up with your own answer and just wait for someone to match it, intending to do what you planned all along. Tricking team members into thinking that they are helping you find a solution to a problem that you have already picked is manipulative and easily spotted. Team members quickly find out that you cannot be trusted.

> Marty, the owner of a successful meat and potato diner in an enclosed shopping mall, had been paying a freelance window trimmer to change the front display twice each month. Her three full-time servers were so critical of the displays that she asked them to decide whether to keep the professional or to rotate the job among themselves. They said they would like to do it themselves. After two months, Marty had to agree that not only were the displays better, but all three servers were better motivated.

Principle 5: Maintain an Open Door Policy

The supervisor who is easy to approach builds better relationships than the aloof supervisor who is difficult to talk with and hard to see. Encourage your team members to come to you freely with suggestions and complaints or for counsel. To allow this communication to happen, you must avoid building physical or psychological barriers between yourself and each team member. Try to establish and practice an open door policy through which free, open, healthy communication practices can be built. Fear or distrust can prevent good communication and hurt relationships. Merely keeping the door to your office open and telling team members to drop by is not enough. You must work to create a nonthreatening atmosphere that will welcome team members to come to you. Seeking them out by walking around and visiting them is an effective strategy for opening doors.

> Ms. Trent was the supervisor of an office staff of 12. Unfortunately, her office was enclosed in glass and visible to all team members. They could not hear Ms. Trent's conferences, but they could observe them. As a result, despite her best efforts, no one wanted to be made conspicuous while talking over problems in the supervisor's office. Her solution was to schedule and conduct short discussions once a month with each team member at a special location in the team member cafeteria. These meetings took time she could ill afford, but they greatly strengthened relationships and productivity increased.

Using the Five Principles

The five principles help the supervisor build and keep healthy, productive relationships with team members. Obviously, these principles are not difficult to understand, nor does it take a supervisor with 20 years of experience to put them into practice. Why, then, are they so frequently taken for granted and so seldom used? Here are three possible reasons:

■ Some ambitious supervisors spend their time seeking more sophisticated methods instead of realizing that these five principles will serve them well.

■ Some supervisors give these foundations lip service by claiming to use them when they do not. They say one thing and do another; only the people they supervise know the truth.

■ Some supervisors accept the principles at face value and honestly try to use them but fail because they do not use them consistently day after day.

How can you sense the need for the five principles and use them naturally in your daily contact with team members? First, you must make a personal commitment, convincing yourself of their value. You must believe they are sound human relations principles. Second, you must incorporate them into your way of working with your team members and integrate them into your daily routine. The more you practice these five principles, the better you become at using them.

THE MICRO LEADER

Micro leadership is defined as tight or close supervision, where every move is watched and monitored by the supervisor. The supervisor does not delegate even simple routine tasks for fear that they will not be done correctly. Many leaders in the hospitality industry tend to be micro or hands-on leaders. Often, micro leaders are frantically running around the establishment carrying the bulk of the workload on their shoulders. Too many leaders work this way because they believe this is how they should work. Our contention is that leaders who have always worked this way do so because they are not effectively managing the facility or they have never been shown a different style of leadership.

The micro leader often has to work this way because his or her staff is not adequately trained or the facility is not adequately staffed. This type of leader leads the operation through his or her efforts. Team members are present to support the leader instead of supporting the operations. The success of the meal period, the rush hour, and so on hinge solely on the efforts of the leader. As a customer, how many meal periods have you witnessed that have long, slow lines and a micro leader was working?

Micro leaders model the performance that team members should mimic but fail to train team members to do what they do. Micro leaders are physically carrying the operation and bearing the full stress of the operations. This type of behavior becomes addictive and difficult to stop. Micro leaders burn out, and they are so prevalent in our industry that we turn over (lose) many capable leaders simply because they wear out. They are simply trying to survive the next meal period, rush hour, or day. No one can work this way for long.

How do you know if you are a micro leader?

■ Unless you are physically working, the operation does not run well.

■ You don't have the right people doing the right job.

■ You feel like you are a victim of "management blackmail" because you have to keep on your staff people that you should fire because you have no one else to replace them.

■ You feel tired, stressed, and maybe despondent most of the time.

■ You spend more time thinking about quitting your job than you focus on doing your job.

■ You work exhausting, long hours with little or no rewards.

■ Your operation is not fully staffed.

■ Your staff is not trained.

■ You are working as hard as you can and you feel like you are on the verge of being fired because you still cannot do everything you have to do.

Micro leaders fail because

■ They burn out their staff. Team members quit because they don't like working in an environment that encourages failure rather than success.

■ They are too busy trying to survive the challenges of the operations to move ahead.

■ They are constantly working in crisis mode.

■ They have no time for planning.

■ They often are scapegoats, or they are fired or forced to quit their jobs due to the failure of the operations.

When a facility is staffed and trained to support the function of the establishment, the micro leader can stop being a hands-on leader. The only time supervisors should be micro leaders is when they are training their staff to do their job or training someone to be a trainer. If you have to become a micro leader for any other reason, you must continue to develop your staff. When your staff can perform the work that you are doing to sustain your operations, they free you to focus your energy and time on directing the operation, improving systems, and creating opportunities to grow sales.

SCHEDULING AND PRODUCTIVITY

The schedule one works directly affects one's overall job motivation and thus affects productivity. Pay, the type of work, and the workload are often affected by the schedule worked. Meeting every employee's scheduling expectations can be a difficult challenge. Flex scheduling, peak periods, and the need to customize job hours for people with special skills is an increasing challenge. Most managers, especially those who utilize part-timers, often prepare weekly printed schedules and post them on a bulletin board. Once printed and posted, the schedule becomes set. Changes are permitted only under exceptional circumstances.

Obviously, restaurants, fast-food operations, retail stores, and organizations that are open extended and irregular hours are presented with the greatest challenge.

Frank operates his highly successful cafe with five full-timers and 20 part-timers. To simplify his work, Frank posts a weekly schedule listing the hours to be worked by each team member. If a part-timer needs to be absent for a shift, it is the team member's responsibility to get a replacement from the list of available part-timers provided, with telephone numbers, by Frank. Frank claims his system works 95% of the time and requires a minimum amount of supervision.

Like Frank, most organizations use their computer capabilities to develop and execute work schedules and patterns to meet their own peculiar needs. Although some supervisors delegate this function, they recognize that the responsibility remains with them and that some flexibility is necessary to keep team members motivated.

CONCLUSION

Supervisors occupy a unique and sometimes contradictory role. Although they must possess the knowledge and skills to do the specific jobs they ask their team members to do, they must refrain from doing these jobs so that they can lead and manage. Supervisors must be content to teach others how to reach their potential. They must reach their own goals through the efforts of others. It takes a special perspective and sensitivity to achieve success in this role. Motivation is internal to human beings. The supervisor can create and maintain an environment of motivation in a variety of ways. Achieving total quality relationships with team members is essential to motivation and high productivity.

DISCUSSION QUESTIONS

1. Why might it be extremely difficult—perhaps impossible—for a worker who has been in a highly skilled job for 10 years to become a successful supervisor?

2. When, if ever, would a supervisor be justified in saying, "It's easier to do it myself"?

3. How will incorporating the five principles of TQR help the supervisor achieve goals?

4. Which of the five principles of TQR would you give top priority? Which one would you give the lowest? Why?

5. What things might supervisors do to create a motivating environment?

6. What are the seven ways to achieve higher productivity?

7. Identify when it would be inappropriate to be a micro leader.

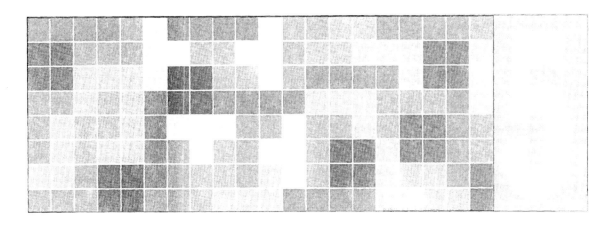

Building Relationships

After you have finished reading this chapter, you should be able to

■ explain the various relationships associated with your job,

■ define 10 ways to help support your team members, and

■ state the disadvantages of giving too close or tight supervision.

If you are going to be a successful leader in the hospitality industry, you have to maintain successful relationships. Developing, nurturing, and maintaining relationships is the key to success in the hospitality industry.

THE RELATIONSHIP WEB

The hospitality industry caters to the needs of people. Your ability to understand, nurture, and maintain relationships creates the foundation for your success.

As a supervisor, you must concurrently manage and understand the dynamics of each of the groups in the relationship web. Each group's needs are different, and your role with each group will be different.

You As Leader

As the supervisor, you must take responsibility for your behavior. You cannot expect others to do anything that you are not doing. You cannot model poor behavior and expect appropriate behavior. You possess a position of influence, and people will respond to what you exhibit to them. Teach people how to treat you by treating them with the candor and respect you expect to have returned to you.

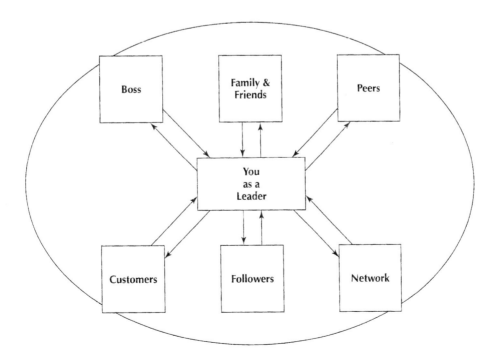

Your Family and Friends

All friendships are relationships, but not all relationships are friendships. Hopefully you will form friendly relationships with your co-workers. As a supervisor, many of the people that report to you will not be your close personal friends. You may not interact with them beyond the workplace. There is a difference between having friendships with the people at work and being friendly to them. How civil and friendly your employees are to you and to one another are important indicators of a healthy team environment.

You must have supportive relationships outside work. Relationships with family and friends are invaluable; protect and nurture these relationships. A balance between work and outside interest is very important, and family and friends can help you maintain that balance.

Your Peers

Some of your success will be dependent on the work efforts of other departments. Maintaining positive rapport with your peers is mutually beneficial. As other departments depend on you to carry out your responsibilities, you will depend on them to exchange the same courtesy. Supportive work relationships with your peers can curtail needless delays and bureaucratic challenges.

Your Boss

For better or worse, everyone has a boss. You have a boss, and you are the boss for your team. You will have to adjust your work habits to synchronize with your supervisor's leadership style.

Your boss expects you to do the following:

- accept responsibility for the performance of your team,

- elevate the performance of your team,

- inform him or her of accomplishments and challenges to operations,

- keep him or her apprised of information/situations affecting his or her area of responsibilities,

- seek approval, guidance, or directions on addressing concerns extending beyond your immediate authority, and

- suggest ideas for improving the effectiveness and efficiency of your operations.

Your Followers

Team members want you to remember where you came from. Most bosses started out working in the position(s) they are now responsible for supervising. The people you supervise want you to empathize with their position. Here is how you can best support your team members:

1. Team members want you to be the boss you wished you had when you were in their position. When you were a team member, you understood the

challenges of your job. You also had an opinion about how management was affecting your ability to work. The people you direct want you to do the same things management did when you were a team member to make you successful and to stop doing what management did to create problems on the job.

2. Team members want you to involve them in decisions that affect them. They want you to realize that they often know the cause and solution to problems that you are trying solve.

3. Team members want you to be willing to listen to them.

4. Team members want you to know that their salary is important to them and they want to be paid a decent wage and work enough hours to meet their objectives. You should know how many hours everyone on your staff needs to work and try to accommodate them even if it means cross training so that they can work enough hours. Helping your staff meet their salary goals enhances relationships. Additionally, when you give salary increases, they need to be substantial enough to be meaningful.

5. Team members want you to pay them based on their performance. Those who perform the best should be paid the most. Good wages and performance incentives will help you build a loyal, productive staff.

6. Team members want you to recognize and reward their performance. You need to know your team members well enough to know what type of recognition/rewards they would like to receive. A good recognition and reward system improves teamwork, outcomes, and efficiency.

7. Team members have other interests besides working for you, so they want you to be flexible. There will be times when you will need to adjust team members' schedules, and there will be times when they will want you to adjust their schedules.

8. Team members spend a lot of time at work. In some cases, they will spend more time on the job than anywhere else. Team members want you to care about them and recognize that the time they spend at work matters. Appreciate their time and make it an enjoyable experience to be at work.

9. Team members want to be successful on the job, so teach them, develop them, and make them successful.

10. Team members want you to know that they are your first customers. How you treat team members directly correlates to how well your paying customers are treated. Make sure you are taking care of all your customers.

Your Network

While there will be times when you feel you are the only one that experiences your challenges and tribulations, don't believe it. Rely on your network, other people in and outside your organization, to keep you grounded. Your network can aid you in improving your knowledge and skills as well as your team's. To expand your network, consider joining trade and professional organizations, attend conferences and training seminars, and develop rapport with people inside and outside your organization.

Your Customers

A fundamental principle of hospitality is to cater to and satisfy the needs of our customers. Today, nearly every organization, whether a four-diamond hotel, a hospital, a manufacturing plant, a grocery, and up-scale department or discount store, a restaurant chain, or even a government agency like the IRS, is concerned about customer service. The story goes that if you build a satisfying relationship with your customers, they will come and, ultimately, so will profits.

Organizations document the importance of customer relations in their vision and mission statements. They train their employees how to listen and how to solve customer problems. Some offer very liberal return policies, and some even hire greeters to meet customers at the door. *Fortune* 500 companies spend billions of dollars every year advertising how dedicated they are to the proposition that all customers are first and foremost in their business plans. As customers, we know good customer treatment when we see it. It feels good to be an important person, to be listened to, to be valued and treated fairly. We truly appreciate superior customer service, and we have come to expect it. What part does leadership of organizations play in building and maintaining first-class customer relations? To what degree are the supervisors of these organizations responsible for creating great customer relationships? How do they sustain a customer-first atmosphere, one practiced consistently throughout the entire organization? How do they inspire their employees to truly value their customers and give that extra measure of concern and courtesy? By treating their employees as well as or better than you treat their customers.

It is that simple. Treat your employees with as much respect and dignity you give to your customers. Truly value your employees by asking for their input into matters that affect them. Give them training and opportunities to develop their skills in all areas of the business. Assume that your employees are honest and treat them accordingly until they prove otherwise. Provide your employees with accurate, timely, and specific feedback on their performance and give them recognition for their contributions to the running of their department. Help them feel ownership of their job through accountability. In other words, let them know that they are first-class members of the organization as a whole and in your area of responsibility specifically.

If you are not treating your employees this way, how can you expect them to do it for a total stranger who walks in the front door of your resort? Employees often give what they get. And as the old saying goes, "If you can't do it for yourself, then you can't do it for the rest of the world." Employees may treat customers better than their supervisor treats them in the short run, but it cannot be sustained.

CONCLUSION

Your ability to understand, nurture, and maintain relationships creates the foundation for your success. As the supervisor, you must take responsibility for your behavior. You cannot expect others to do anything that you are not doing. A balance between work and outside interests is very important, and family and friends can help you maintain that balance. Supportive work relationships with your peers can curtail needless delays and bureaucratic challenges. The people you supervise want you to empathize with their position. Rely on your network, other people in and outside your organization, to keep you grounded. Your network can aid you in improving your knowledge and skills as well as your team's.

DISCUSSION QUESTIONS

1. How can the hospitality industry save leaders from being burned out?

2. Why is it important for you to develop your relationship with your family and friends? Your peers? Your boss?

3. How does the following work environment affect team members' morale, staffing turnover, sales, and productivity of a restaurant?
   - The restaurant has incapable team members and an incapable leader.
   - The restaurant has incapable team members and a capable leader.
   - The restaurant has capable team members and an incapable leader.
   - The restaurant has capable team members and a capable leader.

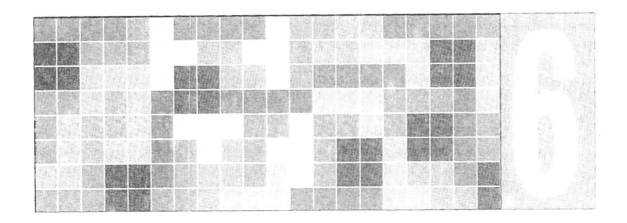

Creating a Productive Work Climate

THE SUPERDUPER SUPERVISOR CLIMATE CONTROL PRODUCTION MAXIMIZER

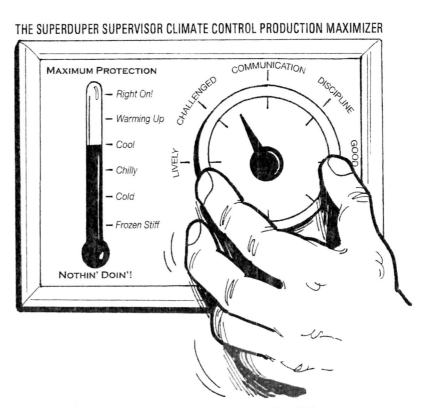

We already have everything we need to be successful. We're just not using it.

After you have finished reading this chapter, you should be able to

- list the steps you would follow to create and maintain a productive working climate,

- describe three lines of discipline supervisors use and explain the criteria for adopting each line, and

- describe how to handle workplace emergencies in a manner that will enforce your authority.

Maintaining a good working climate requires attention. You must work at it daily by contributing new ideas and lively comments, injecting a little humor to keep team members reacting in positive ways, inserting some deserved compliments to help motivate people, and, above all, communicating. Obviously, you must do a great deal of experimenting before coming up with a satisfactory climate. Do not expect immediate results. Even after you have achieved a good climate, it is not easily maintained. Constant work is required. However, the supervisor who eventually does create and maintain an effective working climate can establish good productivity records and enhance his or her personal progress.

DEVELOPING THE RIGHT CLIMATE BY EXAMPLE

The example set by the supervisor contributes more than anything else to establishing your work environment. The speed at which you work sets a tempo for others. Most of your team members expect you to set standards through your personal behavior. They observe your every move: how you respond to customers and answer the telephone, the speed at which you work, and the way you communicate to team members.

One of your team members can afford a bad day, but you cannot; one of your workers can get by with a grouchy attitude, but you cannot; one of your subordinates can let you down, but you cannot. You are the leader, and as such you must consistently set the best possible example. It is the price you pay for accepting a leadership role.

Maintaining a Lively Climate

Lighten the climate with a sense of humor. It is easy for the supervisor, weighed down with many responsibilities, to become too serious about the job. When that happens, a cloud of gloom may settle over the environment. The sensitive manager, seeing this situation beginning to develop, will break it up with a little fun or appropriate humor and lighten up the mood. Take James' situation as an example.

James operated a highly successful fast food franchise. Most of his team members were part-time high school and college students. Knowing that he could pay only minimum wages but needing dependability and high performance, he did every thing possible to make the work fun and build team spirit among the team members. After the store was closed, his team members would play their favorite music over the public address system. They danced and sang along—so did James. His comment to me was, "It is nothing more than a human relations safety valve that permits everyone to let their hair down harmlessly for a short period. It releases the pressure and helps me keep the working climate I need to be successful."

Team members, generally speaking, have a more positive attitude when they are busy completing worthwhile tasks. Idle workers usually become bored and eventually negative. By keeping team members busy through advanced planning and delegating, the supervisor will create a more positive work climate and reach higher levels of productivity. The most difficult job in the world is one in which a team member has too little to do. The effective manager will see that no such jobs exist under his or her direction.

Communications Daily

The most disastrous thing you can do as a supervisor is to break off communications with your people. This breakdown usually happens when supervisors get so busy with reports, planning, projects, meetings, and other activities that they stay hidden in their offices too long. Loss of communication—for any reason—will destroy morale and productivity faster than anything else. Because of this concern, some managers force themselves to get away from their other responsibilities once each day for the purpose of casual communications with their team members. It is a sound practice. Regularly scheduled team meetings, led by the supervisor, demonstrate commitment to open communication.

Handling Emergencies

The way you handle emergencies shows your real character more than normal circumstances do. If you lose your cool under stress, the security of those who work for you will be seriously undermined. Take Barbra, for example.

> Barbra was recently hired to manage a conference center located on a busy street in a major city. She had more than 10 men and 20 women working for her, and she knew that she was being tested in many ways. The staff had not yet accepted her. One day an automobile crashed through the front window, caught fire, and created general chaos. She acted quickly. She used the fire extinguisher to put out the fire, had one of her staff call 911, and made sure all her team members were okay. Barbra handled the situation calmly, efficiently, and without losing her head. From that moment on, she was fully accepted as part of the staff.

Barbra's behavior under stress demonstrated her leadership and gave the staff the security it needed. As a result, the work climate became more relaxed and productivity increased. You cannot make up a fake emergency to enhance your image with your staff, but if one comes along, do not panic; follow procedures and involve others in decisions.

Team member mistakes may create some of these emergencies, and the way you react to them is important. Nothing is more deflating to the ego or more embarrassing than to make a stupid mistake in front of others. Yet we all do it occasionally. The way you react to such mistakes by your staff members will greatly affect the climate you are attempting to build. Take Carlos, for example.

Carlos was named general manager of a very popular coffee shop. He had been in charge only two days when Hazel, carrying a large, heavy tray of gourmet coffee beans, slipped on the newly polished floor and spilled everything. After helping Hazel to her feet, Carlos calmly got down on his knees and helped retrieve the many beans. He showed no anger, no disgust, and no impatience; in fact, he asked one of the other women to take Hazel to the team members' room while he cleaned and set up her beverage station. As a result, everybody relaxed and Carlos was well on his way to establishing a healthy, productive working climate.

Team members are sensitive to the way a fellow team member is treated, and when Carlos built a good relationship with Hazel, he enhanced his relationships with the rest of his staff.

Absorbing Pressures

The way you handle pressures from above also affects the work climate. Every supervisor is occasionally on the receiving end of certain demands from people in higher positions. When such a demand is made, you may react in one of these ways:

- You can pass the pressure on by calling a staff meeting and chewing everybody out, or

- You can absorb as much of the pressure as possible without passing it on.

Here's the way Steve, an operations manager for the atrium section of a large convention center in a popular metropolitan city, reacted.

It was Steve's first job as a supervisor, and in his anxiety to accomplish many things in the first two weeks, he had neglected to have his staff do the necessary cleaning of the atrium. As a result, the atrium section was dirty and messy. Predictably, a high-level manager made a routine inspection late one afternoon and reprimanded Steve privately—and emphatically—for the condition of his area. Although he was emotionally upset and was tempted to chew out his staff (after all, it was their fault), he absorbed the pressure and said nothing that day. The following morning Steve discovered his staff was busy cleaning things up. Apparently, someone had heard the reprimand Steve had received and passed the word along. Steve never had to say a word to his staff. They respected his willingness to take a reprimand on their behalf without passing it on. From then on, Steve had little trouble keeping the atrium clean.

Communicating Changes

The way you react and communicate changes to your staff is critical to a productive working climate. Changes constitute a challenge to the supervisor. In fact, organizational changes are the source of most pressures felt by management and nonmanagement alike. The better you are at adjusting to change, the easier it will be for your team members to accept changes and the more productive your working climate will be. Even more important is the manner in which you communicate forthcoming changes to your team members.

Doreen received word Friday evening after all of her team members had left for the weekend that her customer service department would be transferred to an older, less desirable building. She took time on Saturday to inspect the new location and worked out a tentative floor plan. She announced the change in a positive way Monday morning and asked team members for input on her plan. Before the day was over everyone had made a good adjustment, and some were looking forward to the additional freedom that would result from moving to the new location.

How can you tell when you have created the ideal work climate? High productivity and quality (measured by sales, customer counts, controllables, satisfaction measurements, staff retention, or service standards) and good team member–manager relationships are good indicators. The characteristics of a poor climate are complaints, human relations problems, absenteeism, team member rip-offs, hostility, errors, and a general lack of enthusiasm. Like a maintenance technician calibrating a thermostat, the leader should occasionally take readings and make adjustments.

DISCIPLINE LINES: PERMISSIVE, INTERMEDIATE, AND TIGHT

The major reasons for the deterioration of formerly productive environments are neglect, failure to alleviate controllable pressures, and an inappropriate discipline line. A supervisor with a high, permissive, or loose discipline line will have more problems when team members lack self-discipline, lack work-related experience, or lack the willingness to take responsibility for their decisions.

How much freedom do you give your team members? At what point do you draw the line? At what point do you respond to team members stepping over the line? Supervisors must seek and find their own line based on their leadership styles and some objective criteria. The line of discipline is the point beyond which team members know they should not push. It defines what team members are permitted to do within the work environment without violating procedures, policy, and working standards.

Different lines may be set differently for each employee and for each working environment. An effective way to determine where to set the line is by assessing the maturity of each team member. Maturity is the product of two factors. The first factor is the employee's ability to do the job. Experience and training affect ability. The second factor is the team member's willingness to take responsibility for his or her decisions. Self-confidence, a track record of accomplishment, and experience in making decisions affect willingness.

A permissive discipline line permits maximum freedom because it calls for a minimum of control or supervision. For the most part, team members are expected to provide self-discipline. A permissive line works best when team members are mature in their positions. Team members who are highly skilled in their work and are highly willing to take responsibility for their behavior can be allowed a permissive line. These are the team members that the supervisor can delegate important tasks to because they can be trusted to deliver.

An intermediate line permits considerable freedom but maintains certain standards that relate to productivity. This type of discipline policy usually works best in retail stores, hotels, or commissaries, where high customer relations standards are maintained but the team members are encouraged to be relaxed and friendly. Bear in mind that the maturity of the team member is the deciding factor, not the nature of the work when determining the appropriate line.

A tight discipline line limits team members' freedom. In some cases, these restrictions are necessary. Tight discipline is appropriate, for example, when team members are new to a job and lack experience or when they lack self-confidence and look for guidance from the supervisor or others before making decisions. A tight line is often appropriate in an environment that employs young workers, like a fast food restaurant.

Supervisors who base their line of discipline on the ability of their team to do the job and on their willingness to take responsibility for their decisions will ensure that the proper line is drawn. You will gain and keep the respect of your team members by establishing the appropriate line. As a team member matures in his or her job, the line can be adjusted accordingly.

> Dave was concerned about how closely his supervisor observed his work. He was constantly checking on him to see if his work was being done. Dave was new to the job, but learning fast was one of his strengths. He noticed that he was the only one being watched this closely. He was concerned about it so he asked his supervisor why he was being treated differently than the others.
>
> His supervisor explained that his line of discipline is based on team members' ability to do the job and their willingness to take responsibility for their decisions. All new employees are held to a tight line until they demonstrate that they can handle the responsibility of a permissive line.
>
> Dave was glad to hear the reason and understood clearly the reason behind his supervisor's behavior.

Setting the appropriate line may also be influenced by the work environment. A tight line might be necessary in highly regulated operations where safety is a paramount concern. A fast-paced kitchen environment may require a tighter line because accidents could cause serious injury or unsanitary conditions could cause food-borne illnesses.

Within each environment many variations will occur. A supervisor, of course, could maintain a low, strong discipline line and still have a positive attitude and friendly atmosphere.

Once you find the right discipline line for your work situation, maintaining it will require daily attention. To illustrate, let's look at three hypothetical situations.

> Rick runs a meat processing plant. The food safety hazards of meat requires extreme adherence to safety guidelines. Rick's line of discipline leaves little room for socializing and a narrow margin for error. The atmosphere is one of strict compliance. An experienced outsider observing the situation senses that the environment might be slightly overcontrolled, overmanaged, and overstructured. The productivity and quality levels are average. A trained observer senses a climate of sternness and conformity. (This type of discipline policy is often called autocratic.)

> Ron, on the other hand, operates a loose environment. In his laundry room he gives his team members more freedom than they know how to handle. The work gets

done, but because of excessive horseplay, occasional errors crop up that must be corrected. Ron feels that team members resent close supervision, so he stays clear except when he feels it necessary to become more involved. The atmosphere is one of noisy relaxation. A trained observer senses an absence of direction. The productivity and quality levels are below average. (This style is often called permissive.)

Susan is following a middle-of-the-road philosophy. She wants her sales staff to have the autonomy they need to attract clients. The discipline line is there, but it is not overpowering and restrictive. She tries not to be too permissive but consciously avoids overcontrol. As a result, she does a balancing act between the two. She strives to create a democratic climate in which team members have a degree of freedom but still welcome her leadership, if and when necessary. To the perceptive outsider, the atmosphere is businesslike, with more than average communication between team members. The productivity and quality levels are above average. (This style is often called democratic.)

Three different lines of disciplines create three different working climates in the preceding scenarios. The discipline line affects the overall work climate and thus is important to overall job satisfaction. An oppressive work climate is just that, oppressive. A permissive climate that is inappropriate for the maturity level of the employee or the nature of the work can be very dangerous.

Consider the following three points about work climate:

1. You must create and maintain your own work climate.

2. The best climate is the one that generates the highest-quality productivity and relationships between team members and their manager.

3. Climates change according to the needs of the environment and its team members.

Compassion and Control

The inexperienced newcomer to supervision may think that it is impossible to demonstrate compassion and maintain a tight discipline line at the same time. Not so. Compassion for others can be communicated in any working climate. In fact, if handled in a sensitive manner, team members may accept a stronger, tighter discipline line from a more compassionate supervisor. Some less permissive supervisors consistently demonstrate that they care deeply for their team. Compassion and tight lines of discipline controls are not contradictory.

ESTABLISHING A CONSISTENT CLIMATE

Err on the side of strong leadership. A strong leader is one who provides the correct balance of control and freedom in his or her area of responsibility. Most team members prefer consistent leadership behavior whether permissive or tight. Being able to predict a supervisor's reaction has a stabilizing effect on team members. Most team members cannot function well in an atmosphere devoid of consistency; they want decisive leadership and work best in a predictable, controlled environment. The fewer rules the better in most situations, but the rules must be clear and set a firm line that all perceive accurately.

> Angelita moved in as the new restaurant district manager quietly and in a warm and friendly manner, but she set a much firmer discipline line than her predecessor. Sales (measured in customer counts) were up 20% the first quarter. Later, some of her managers told her what it was like to work under the previous district manager: "I didn't feel like I was being held accountable for anything"; "There was little recognition in doing good work."; "I feel like we have a plan of action under your supervision"; and "If there is anything that frustrates me, it's a boss who doesn't enforce their expectations."

Maintain Consistency

Find the ideal climate for your environment and then maintain it. Be consistent in the way you treat your team members and predictable in the way you handle your duties. Daily fluctuations in expectations keep everyone on edge; they are confusing and hold productivity down. Team members want to know what to expect.

> Raymond, the sandwich shop owner, set his line of discipline on a daily basis. When he was in a good mood, he was extremely friendly and tolerant (raising the line); when he was in a serious mood, he was stern and demanding (lowering the line). In less than two months, he had lost two team members, and two others had given notice. When asked why, one replied, "He expects us to adjust to his mood every day, and we never know which Raymond is coming to work today—we never know what to expect. He's inconsistent and unpredictable. It's worse than dealing with your own children." Another team member said, "Once you get used to the rules, he changes them in a capricious manner that leaves me disturbed and angry. I would prefer a less capable but more consistent manager."

Seek Feedback from Your Team

One way to get feedback from your staff is to mingle a little with your team members during breaks. If the timing seems right, ask how things are going and then listen to the responses you receive. Be open to their feedback. If you are trusted, you may hear complaints or compliments. If you receive few complaints, you probably have the kind of climate you want; if you receive many complaints, things must be out of balance, and you should adjust your discipline line. It is easier to make small adjustments to a working climate than to make major repairs. If you listen to team members' complaints and value their input, you may receive information that leads to greater productivity.

Fine-Tune Your Line of Discipline

When adjustments are made, make them gently. Maintaining the right discipline line takes sensitive maneuvering. The manager who overreacts one way or the other often must start from scratch. Here is a classic example.

About three months ago, things were going well in Carl's environment. Production was high and morale was great. Apparently Carl had come up with the perfect climate, so he relaxed and became more permissive. He felt he could trust his staff. Two weeks later, things began to go wrong. Productivity dropped and mistakes increased. Carl, overreacting, moved in and tightened the discipline line harshly and emotionally, resulting in even lower productivity. Team members didn't want to work hard for someone who gave them freedom one day and took it away the next. Carl needed to learn that sudden, drastic adjustments to his discipline line could easily boomerang. The best policy is to take frequent observations and make minor adjustments.

When it comes to enforcing rules, safety regulations, and compliance with the law, there is no room for inconsistency. These items exist to maintain the welfare of the workplace and to protect every team member. For the most part, team members will discipline themselves to comply with these items. However, when incidents of deviant behavior occur and these items are violated, a swift, consistent, and firm response is required. Your responsibility is to protect all team members through enforcement of the guidelines. Sometimes that means protecting team members from themselves, and it always means protecting and enforcing your line of discipline.

CONCLUSION

Maintaining a good working climate requires attention. The example set by the supervisor contributes more than anything else to establishing your work environment. Generally speaking, employees have a more positive attitude when they are busy doing worthwhile tasks. The most disastrous thing you can do as a supervisor is to break off communications with your people. The way you react and communicate changes to your staff is critical to a productive working climate. Supervisors are responsible for setting the appropriate line of discipline. A permissive line, an intermediate line, or a tight line may be based on team member maturity and on the nature of the work. Once you find the right discipline line for your work situation, maintaining it will require daily attention.

DISCUSSION QUESTIONS

1. Explain the criteria for setting a permissive line of discipline.

2. Explain the criteria for setting a tight line of discipline.

3. Team member maturity is determined by what two factors?

4. What are some common mistakes that supervisors make regarding discipline?

5. Describe how your line of discipline can affect the work climate.

6. How does your line of discipline help build relationships between you and your team members?

7. What are some ways to create a positive working climate?

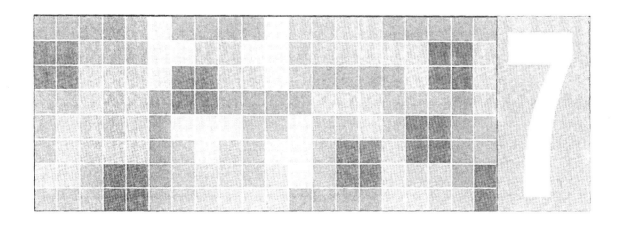

Helping Your Staff
Become a Team

People want to be on a team. They want to be part of something bigger than themselves. They want to be in a situation where they feel that they are doing something for the greater good.

Mike Krzyzewski
Duke University Basketball Coach

After you have finished reading this chapter, you should be able to

- communicate the essential differences between a traditional department and a contemporary team arrangement,

- operate successfully with team members from diverse cultural backgrounds,

- define the personal characteristics needed by a team leader, and

- talk about the three service roles in team meetings.

We live in a time of uncertainty. Now more than ever we seek reassurance from our leaders, only to find that too often our confidence is shaken as we are bombarded with news of corporate corruption, financial distortions, and imperial destruction of companies with brand names as familiar as America itself.

The future is unclear. A major restructuring of companies is taking place in the United States. Downsizing, thinning out of middle management positions, and greater international involvements are in progress. These and other unsettling changes are necessary to enable companies to position themselves for longevity, generate higher sales, and grow a customer base in an effort to remain competitive. It is the hospitality challenge of the century!

FROM "THEM" TO "US"

The traditional department with authority and responsibility held tightly by management is giving way to a more productive team approach. The team concept is not new; it has been around for a long time and tried under many formulas. Naturally, some companies are more suited to adopt the team approach than others. The basic trend, however, is gaining momentum. The supervisor of the future will be prepared as a team leader as much as a departmental manager. Why will this preparation be prevalent? Because when team members get swept up in a well-led team project, they become more involved. Personal involvement in decision making can produce higher levels of both quantity and quality. As a result, everyone benefits.

> When Dora accepted an offer from a more progressive casual dining operation, she was warned that as a manager she would need to absorb and apply the team philosophy endorsed by the new president. She accepted the challenge and immediately started to learn as much about the team approach as possible. Dora knew it would mean sharing the authority she previously enjoyed, more frequent communication, added patience so that each team member could be involved in major decisions, and a variety of other changes. In fact, she would need to revamp her behavioral patterns and style as a manager. For the first 30 days, things were bumpy and, on a few occasions, chaotic.

At times, Dora was tempted to fall back on her old command-and-control approach, but she resisted. She wisely recognized that she could be sending a mixed message to team members by oscillating between the two organizational styles. This inconsistency could cause confusion and lower productivity. Instead, she accepted suggestions from other team leaders (fellow supervisors), and everything started to come together. When asked by her superior how she was doing, Dora replied, "I still feel a little insecure and I still haven't been able to shed all of my previous habits, but all team members are responding and I am more excited about my job than ever before."

BECOMING A BOUNDARY LEADER

In making the transition, it may help traditional managers to think of themselves as boundary managers instead of direct, forceful bosses. A team leader acts as a facilitator and public relations agent, and a coach. The leader spends more time coordinating operations efforts with other departments, obtaining resources the team needs, and negotiating conflicts inside and outside team boundaries.

A team boundary is the sphere of responsibility or the work area of the team. A boundary leader is needed when a problem transcends the team's boundary. The team hands off the problem to the boundary leader, and he or she takes it from there. The sharing of authority once held only by the supervisor can sometimes cause a leader to feel isolated and ineffective. Should these feelings arise, the leader might mistakenly return to the old style.

In previous chapters, you studied the fundamentals involved in creating good relationships as a traditional supervisor. You may not have been aware that everything you learned is even more applicable in becoming a team leader. In fact, you will realize that everything you have absorbed, once put into practice, would make you a successful coach. This capability can be significant to your future because of the following trends:

- a steady movement away from the traditional pyramid company structure to the circle or team arrangement;

- increased empowerment, which means that team members are given more autonomy to make decisions, take action, and enhance their own roles; and

- the changing ethnic composition of units, which is becoming more representative of all domestic and international cultures.

BEING AN EFFECTIVE TEAM LEADER

What does one do to become an effective team leader? Here are a few suggestions.

- Delegate more authority and responsibility to all team members; they will feel that they are involved and true members of the team.

- Encourage risk taking and experimentation. Within bounds, let members make mistakes without coming down hard on them. When mistakes happen, help every team member learn from them.

- Develop a shared vision. By being a good listener, you will be better able to help the team develop goals that everyone wants to reach. Then make sure that the rewards are shared equally.

- Keep the team informed; give them information about things important to the team's duties, responsibilities, and opportunities.

- Set the stage for team problem solving. You create a problem-solving atmosphere by taking the time to bring everyone close to the problem so that they can contribute to and accept the consequences of the decision.

- Invite self-expression and open discussion even if it involves conflict. This approach can eliminate feelings of resentment that often cause members to tighten up and cooperate only superficially.

- Run team meetings regularly in order to engage in the preceding activities as a team.

Building a work team is similar to putting a winning basketball team into competition. It does not happen in a few weeks. Sometimes it takes two or three seasons. When total empowerment is accomplished, the results are obvious. The total team power is measurably greater than that previously exercised by each individual player. It is this added dimension that creates a winner.

At the beginning, Dora didn't fully understand all the benefits of empowerment. For example, every time the corporate office sent a new program to the hotel Dora felt that her workload increased. She didn't understand that although she was responsible for all the work being completed, that didn't mean that she had to do all the work. At the suggestion of her supervisor, Dora asked three of her team members to help her with the new program. After assigning each team member specific duties to complete, Dora was able to complete the rollout of the new program in record time.

Dora learned that

- she could execute better her responsibilities by empowering her team members,

- she could help her team members be successful and feel like part of a winning team,

- being involved with a winning team could increase the self-esteem of all players, and

- being involved would increase their contribution in new, creative ways.

Dora didn't realize that empowerment could convert a worker into a more dynamic participant who was willing to work for the team goal with more enthusiasm and dedication. With her new approach, Dora found herself communicating more frequently on an informal level, compromising more to accommodate team members who had demonstrated higher personal productivity. Most of all, she noticed a better learning climate emerging. Everyone wanted to know how they might contribute more in different areas and what they needed to learn to make it possible. When Dora reviewed the sales and customer count, the bottom line showed that the new approach was working. "Wow!" Dora said to herself, "By giving up some of my control and authority, I have empowered myself along with other team members."

Personal Characteristics Required by a Team Leader

What are the personal characteristics of a successful team leader? Patience, having a positive attitude toward team operations, a willingness to listen, flexibility, a desire to inspire, and many other traits are important. However, the number one skill is sensitivity. It takes a light, insightful touch to mold a group of strangers, potentially from different cultures, into a viable, productive team. It takes a perceptive individual who understands group dynamics and can lead without pushing. Such a leader must have compassion for all people and a deep desire to help each individual reach his or her potential as a team member.

A team leader also needs the ability to help members develop a mutual respect for the efforts of each member. Some people refer to mutual respect as the glue that holds a good team together.

A personal characteristic that should be near the top of any list is a sense of humor. A team that cannot relax now and then is a team in name only. When a team achieves a goal, a "reward party" is in order; when a team suffers a defeat, some laughter is needed to enable everyone to learn from the past and begin again. A perceptive leader (or coach) knows that sometimes it is necessary to encourage relaxation to prepare for the next effort.

LEADING THE MULTICULTURAL TEAM

The movement from the pyramid to the circle and team empowerment becomes more intriguing when the international composition of the hospitality industry is introduced. The predominantly homogeneous team of the past is being replaced with an enticing mix of gender, age, race, and cultural backgrounds. Even now, it is not unusual to find five or more different cultures represented in a team of 10 workers.

How does the team leader deal with this challenge? It is primarily a matter of attitude. If the leader views a multicultural team as an unwelcome challenge, problems will compound. If the leader perceives the new mix as an opportunity to utilize a larger pool of talent to further empower the team, relationships will be friendly and productivity will increase. Here are a few techniques that will assist those team leaders who prefer the positive view:

■ Learn from one another. Team member relationships can be strengthened as each individual learns to appreciate and enjoy the culture of another. Free and open communication encouraged by the team leader will help this happen.

■ Some team leaders may think it inappropriate to ask new members from a different culture to discuss their backgrounds and work experience in a different environment. Done properly, however, such discussions could build stronger interpersonal relationships as well as avoid needless misunderstandings. Each culture has differences that affect work behavior. Thus, when a team member knows how a member from a different culture sees the world, the give-and-take can be enhanced. For example, some cultures are more patriarchal than ours, making it natural for workers from these backgrounds to sit back and wait for the boss to give orders rather than move into team efforts on their own.

A new team member—especially if his or her culture has not previously been represented—needs and should receive special support and training from the team leader. This extra effort by the manager can set the tone for other members, and everyone benefits.

- The leader should discover and value the special talents the new member brings to the team and see that those talents are made known and used, inviting collaboration between the seasoned members and the new individual.

- The team leader or manager plays an important role in helping those from foreign cultures learn team protocol. Until newcomers accept the procedures and courtesies normally practiced, they will not find the work environment congenial. As a result, they will not make their full contribution to the team.

- Strong, productive teams are built around strong relationships that are mutually rewarding. That is, all members need to benefit from the presence of each other. Should the leader discover that a misunderstanding or conflict exists, immediate counseling of those involved is recommended. A team is most effective when members are compatible and each relationship is mutually rewarding.

Your attitude toward the multicultural team structure is very important. Do you want a team made up of persons from diverse cultures, or is management mandating it? Are you free of prejudice so that fair treatment is guaranteed? Do you bring the full potential of each member so that long-term goals can be reached to the surface? Are you willing to accept the challenges inherent in forming a model multicultural team?

When Janelle took over the international culinary department in her hospitality business school, she was not surprised about the mix of men and women or the different age levels. It did surprise her, however, to realize that she had one Asian, one Hispanic, two African Americans, one Romanian, and one Arab in her department. Obviously, her new department had an international flavor well beyond that of her previous experiences. Did the mix make Janelle's job more difficult? At the beginning, yes. She had to remind herself that the most basic and important principle of human relationships is to treat everyone as an individual. It would be her job to ensure that each member received the full respect of all others. Building healthy, open, and compatible interpersonal relationships would be her goal.

After a full month, Janelle had learned more than the identities of the members of the team she had inherited. She discovered, for example, that it was the goal of the team that really brought them together. All she needed to do was work hard herself, teach others by drawing on her greater store of knowledge, communicate a lot, compliment a lot, and keep the team apprised of the progress being made. She learned that regardless of a person's ethic or cultural background they basically wanted the same things from work: a fair wage, a sense of accomplishment and appreciation for their contributions, and a leader who values them as members of the team.

When Janelle discovered that the team concept was a top-priority goal of her new school and that all team leaders met in seminars on a regular basis, she was delighted. This environment would give her the support and skills she would need to survive as a leader in the future. All this activity confirmed that she had made the right decision to join her new employer.

TEAM MEMBER EMPOWERMENT

Empowerment is the key term when it comes to developing an effective team. Under the team umbrella, you give members more power to operate freely, more space to be creative, and more chances to contribute to productivity in their own way. Under the pyramid structure, the manager draws the line; under the team structure, members usually draw their own lines. When these freedoms mesh with reality, the team member is empowered to make the team more productive. In other words, rejoicing over the success of the team is more rewarding than making personal progress at the expense of others. Rewards are better when shared with others who have also contributed.

Fundamentals of an Effective Service Team

In order for teams to perform successfully, members need to be aware of and practice the fundamentals of teamwork. First, the team should meet on a regular basis at a specified time. Teams that do not meet or miss meetings routinely do not perform well. Research on team dynamics indicates that three service roles must be filled during team meetings:

1. Leader

2. Recorder

3. Observer

Each role carries specific responsibilities that affect team dynamics. Except for the leader's role, having team members volunteer to fill each role is often more desirable than appointing someone who may not want it.

The Leader's Role

In most cases, the supervisor of the operations fills the leader's role. In self-led teams, the leader role may rotate among the team members. In both cases, the leader of the team assumes the following responsibilities:

- ensures that team members perform task and maintenance functions and reduces nonfunctional behavior,

- assists the team in choosing and focusing on its tasks and goals,

■ encourages free expression and balanced participation,

■ helps team members listen to each other,

■ helps the team manage conflict, and

■ communicates concerns of the team to the next level of management.

One person or leader does not accomplish all these outcomes easily. In an effective team, each member shares responsibility for performing tasks and maintenance behaviors and for minimizing dysfunctional behaviors. In less mature teams the accountability for these behaviors falls on the leader. The following chart describes each of these behaviors in detail. Dysfunctional behaviors should be addressed immediately.

In an advanced and experienced work team, members usually discipline themselves in order to achieve and maintain group acceptance. A team that normally operates in unison can exert peer pressure on an errant member. Often the leader can remain an observer. When this passive observance does not work, the leader needs to move quickly and quietly to confront the behavioral problem before the individual loses face by disrupting team progress.

Team members need to be confronted privately about their behavior when it jeopardizes the team. Clear expectations for what is expected and the conse-

TEAM BEHAVIORS

Task Behaviors	Maintenance Behaviors	Dysfunctional Behaviors
Beginning: Proposing tasks, goals, or action; defining group problems; suggesting a procedure	**Peace-making:** Attempting to settle disagreements; reducing conflict; getting people to explore differences	**Aggression:** Lowering others' status; attacking the group or its values; joking in a nasty or hurtful way
Informing: Presenting facts; giving expression of feeling; offering an opinion	**Gate keeping:** Helping others to participate; keeping communication channels open	**Blocking:** Disagreeing and opposing beyond "reason"; resisting stubbornly the group's wish for personally oriented reasons; using hidden agenda to stop the movement of the group
Exploring others' ideas: Asking for opinions, facts, and feelings	**General agreement:** Asking whether a group is near a decision; testing a possible conclusion	
Clarifying: Interpreting ideas; asking questions in an effort to understand or promote understanding; saying things in another way	**Encouraging:** Being friendly, warm, and responsive to others; indicating an interest in others' contributions (by facial expressions or remark)	**Dominating:** Asserting authority or superiority to control the group or certain members; interrupting contributions of others; controlling by means of flattery or other forms of insincere behavior

TEAM BEHAVIORS *(continued)*		
Task Behaviors	**Maintenance Behaviors**	**Dysfunctional Behaviors**
Coordinating/ Summarizing: Pulling together related ideas; restating suggestions; offering a decision or conclusion for group to consider	**Compromising:** Giving up part of a personal idea to settle conflict; willingness to change to keep group together	**Out-of-field behavior:** Making a display of one's lack of involvement; seeking recognition in ways not related to group tasks
Reality testing: Making a critical analysis of an idea; testing an idea against some data; trying to see whether the idea would work		**Special interest:** Using the group as a vehicle for outside interests; putting one's beliefs and needs ahead of group needs

Source: Adapted from John McKinley, *Group Development Through Participation Training* (New York; Paulist Press, 1978).

quences for failing to perform as expected should be explained thoroughly. If the behavior persists, the person may need to be disciplined formally or removed from the team.

The Recorder's Role

The recorder performs an important function for the team during team meetings. Primarily the recorder is the note taker during meetings and is responsible for

- providing the team with written documentation of the ongoing discussion by recording comments on an easel or board for all the team to see,

- asking for clarification of ideas or statements as necessary, and

- participating in group discussion but primarily focusing on recording team members' discussion.

Team discussion frequently ebbs and flows. Depending on the nature of the topic, the discussion may prompt many ideas, thoughts, or suggestions to roll out quickly and randomly. The recorder is responsible for capturing key words or phrases during the discussion. This transcription allows the discussion to progress to other thoughts without losing what has been said or suggested. Some team members may require more think time than others to express their thoughts on a subject or idea. Having a written record in front of them provides the opportunity to refer to an earlier statement on the flip chart. An illuminating thought might emerge that was missed the first time. Skills for a recorder include being a good listener and summarizer.

The Observer's Role

The observer is like a mirror that reflects team behavior back to the team members. The reflection is open for investigation and discussion. To accomplish this task, the observer

- provides the team with observations of its behaviors and processes,

- makes comments that are group directed and does not refer to the participants by name in the feedback (at least not in early discussions),

- reports observations at times specified by the leader,

- sits where he or she can see most team members, and

- reports what he or she observed, not what he or she thinks occurred or should have occurred.

The observer should be allotted a specified amount of time during the team meeting to discuss his or her observations. The team may use a formal questionnaire for assessing team behavior, or your team can design its own questionnaire. Using a questionnaire specifically designed for your team is often the most rewarding approach. A typical team climate questionnaire focuses on evaluating teamwork. Instructions direct each team member to evaluate the team's effectiveness in key areas. All individual scores can be averaged and compared to one another.

After completing this feedback form, the team discusses its scores. Goals for correcting weaknesses can be set and the team may wish to celebrate its strengths and accomplishments. Being a member of a fully functioning and effective team is highly rewarding. The cohesive team, effectively led, often outproduces the most productive individual working alone. Making and keeping a team effective requires the constant diligence of each member. Your team's collective behavior will determine how effective your team actually is. Research has shown that teams exhibiting the following seven behaviors (or normative conditions) are most likely to be effective.

1. **Shared planning:** The team decides how it will work to accomplish the goals and objectives set forth by management.

2. **Shared decision making through consensus:** Each team member must be motivated to carry out the decisions of the team and agree that the following three conditions have been met when making decisions.

   a. I have heard and understood all viewpoints expressed.

   b. My viewpoints have been heard and understood by team members.

   c. I am motivated to carry out whatever decision the team makes.

3. **Shared leadership:** The special responsibility of the leader is to perform group task and group maintenance behaviors. Leadership is a set of behaviors, not an individual.

4. **Shared evaluation:** The group assesses the process of its discussions, not just the product of them. The observer role provides feedback to the group on the process, and the group must discuss this feedback.

5. **Two-way communication:** Group members actively listen to what is said and to what is not said, as well as attend to behavior.

6. **Mutual trust:** Participants interact in ways that support the feelings of others as worthy persons, even at times of open disagreement.

7. **Voluntary participation:** Each person must accept responsibility for his or her own actions and for maintaining group conditions that support the personal integrity of the other participants.

Source: Adapted from John McKinley, *Group Development through Participation Training* (New York: Paulist Press, 1978).

CONCLUSION

Some new managers will discover that they have joined a company that promotes and supports the team approach. In these companies, supervisors should, like Janelle, make the transition as soon as it is comfortable to do so.

For those supervisors who join firms that have had little or no experience with teams (as is often the case in small companies), the traditional or pyramid approach is recommended. This environment does not mean, however, that you cannot build a working and productive team within the pyramid structure. Many innovative leaders have discovered that the difference between a department and a team is primarily the kind of leadership provided. You can be called a manager by any company and still develop and lead an effective team even though you receive little help and encouragement from above. If your style of supervision favors the team concept, move with confidence in that direction.

DISCUSSION QUESTIONS

1. List the key components driving many companies in the hospitality industry to abandon their traditional management approach to more of a team approach.

2. What are the advantages of a diverse labor market?

3. What should a team leader do to overcome cultural differences between team members?

4. How do you change a traditional leader into a team leader?

5. Describe a work environment that would best be served by a traditional leader. Defend your answer.

6. What are the characteristics of an effective team leader?

7. Discuss the roles of leader, recorder, and observer in team meetings.

PART III

LEADING
FOR PEAK
PERFORMANCE

Managers must possess strong interpersonal skills. These skills are especially important when dealing with performance issues. In this part we address how to use your interpersonal and communication skills to deal with performance issues such as poor productivity and high turnover.

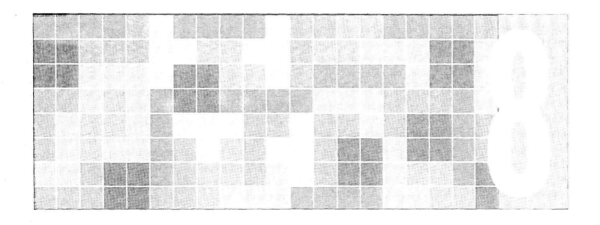

Private Communications

There are times when public behavior or performance must be addressed privately.

After you have finished reading this chapter, you should be able to

- list the five conditions under which private communications can be effective,

- apply the techniques to an actual situation,

- discuss the five R's of communication, and

- discuss why private communications should be linked to individual goals.

THE SUPERVISOR AS COMMUNICATOR

Studies on leadership demonstrate the importance of communication in carrying out job-related responsibilities. On average, supervisors spend 80% of their day communicating with their team employees. Explaining changes, answering questions, providing feedback on performance issues, conducting meetings, training, interviewing new applicants, conducting disciplinary conferences, and orienting new team members are a few of the many important communication activities carried out by the supervisor. Communication plays such a big part in the supervisor's duties that becoming an expert communicator is a must.

Stop for a moment to think about all the communication acts you or your supervisor perform in a day's time and you will readily agree that effective communication is at the heart of sound leadership.

THE SUPERVISOR AS COUNSELOR

Sometimes supervisors are called on to provide counseling to their employees. Performance may be slipping, and your direct reports may need to be informed of a problem in their behavior. It could be something obvious like being late for work or not following standard procedures when carrying out a task. Sometimes the problem is more subtle, like one's overall attitude toward one's work. Or the necessity to counsel may be initiated by your employees and have nothing at all to do with work. Because they respect you, your followers may seek you out for advice on personal matters.

The first step in most disciplinary procedures is often called a counseling session. Its purpose is to allow the supervisor to bring a performance problem to the attention of the employee. Together they talk about the problem and find a way to resolve it. Information gathering, clarification, and problem solving are its intended outcome.

Whether the supervisor initiates the session because of a performance problem or the employee asked to talk privately about a non–work-related issue, the supervisor must keep in mind some important guidelines. Supervisors are not professionally trained or educated counselors. So do not be tempted to play one and provide such services. Supervisors can provide useful input and constructive feedback during private communication sessions. Potentially serious work-related problems can be solved before they escalate; employees can discover important insights into their personal problems when the supervisor cares enough about his or her followers to take the time and effort to hear them out. If you find yourself in one of these private sessions, remember these tips:

1. Counseling sessions are best given in private unless the disciplinary procedure requires a witness to be present. Generally a witness is needed in the advanced stages of the disciplinary procedure. In other cases, such as during the initial stage of the disciplinary procedure or when a non–work-related issue is to be discussed, a private setting in a quiet place is recommended.

2. Focus your initial discussion on the symptoms of the problem and not on finding a solution. Do not jump to solutions or offer them. Try to understand the problem yourself and help your employee to do likewise. It is tempting to give solutions before fully understanding the situation. Sometimes the other person does not want a fix to the problem; he or she just needs someone to listen.

3. Pay attention to the talk:listen ratio. This ratio represents the balance or amount of listening and talking. If you seek first to understand, then you will listen more and talk less. Ask questions for clarification, paraphrase for understanding, but do not dominate the conversation. Even if you are discussing a performance problem, listen to your follower's explanation for his or her behavior.

4. Remember that a great way to teach your employees to listen to you and to one another is by listening to them. Model effective listening, especially during private sessions.

5. Confidentiality is crucial to trust. Trust can be lost if someone makes public what was intended to be kept private. Set the ground rules up front and stick to them. One common example may be to agree that "what is said in the room stays in the room." If at any time something is said that you think must be told to another, tell this to the person confiding in you before the conversation continues. Otherwise keep the conversation confidential.

Supervisors may be confronted with a scenario similar to the following:

Roy is worried. He is having trouble at work. He's been late a couple of times lately; his productivity has been dropping because he finds it hard to concentrate. He knows his supervisor is noticing these changes. Until recently Roy had been a model employee. He could be trusted to carry out his responsibilities with little or no supervision.

Roy's problems at work are a carryover from his home troubles. Roy's wife, Mary, has been drinking again and has become abusive to him and their two young daughters. Taking the girls to school is the reason why he's been late to work. He has been asked to meet with a teacher at school to discuss a problem she is having with his youngest. The meeting is scheduled for this Friday afternoon. Roy will have to ask to leave work early. Friday is not a good day to be asking off since a big banquet is planned.

Deep in thought about his situation, Roy is brought back to the present when his supervisor asks if they could meet privately today at 2:00 P.M.

Roy checks the clock on the wall and exactly at 2:00 P.M., feeling very tired, knocks on his boss's door.

Roy has a serious situation that needs immediate attention. Dealing with Roy's problem requires skills and resources beyond those possessed by his boss.

Roy's boss is well advised to direct Roy to other resources in or outside the company. One resource that may be provided internally is an employee assistance program (EAP). Many organizations provide this type of benefit, usually at no cost to employees, because they realize that sometimes employees need professional counseling services in dealing with personal life issues. Roy's case is a prime example. After listening to Roy's situation, his boss could suggest he use the company's EAP to sort out his problem. If the organization does not have an EAP, the supervisor may suggest one of several community-based resources. Most counties in the United States have a mental health association that can provide a list of helping agencies available to assist its residents. Often the services are paid through tax revenue and therefore are affordable for most budgets.

Structure of Counseling Sessions

The structure of private sessions varies widely. Sometimes a long heart-to-heart talk is needed to clear the air. Sometimes a quick exchange will clear up a misunderstanding.

Private communication sessions are not designed to solve personal or psychological problems. As a supervisor, you are not a psychiatrist, a psychologist, or a professional counselor, but you can counsel team members in your company in order to create and maintain relationships affecting your productivity. *Remember, don't play doctor.*

Meeting privately with your employees usually takes place under one of two circumstances:

- the team member voluntarily comes to the manager with a suggestion, problem, or grievance,

    or

- the supervisor intervenes to motivate a team member, correct a problem, or forestall a grievance.

The supervisor has the advantage when the team member initiates the discussion. For one thing, it means the open door policy is working and confidence has been established. Even when the team member approaches in a hostile mood, the supervisor should welcome the communication because talking things over may be the only safety valve available. Most of the time, team members will approach the supervisor without hostility. The climate will then be relaxed and nonthreatening to both parties. These informal sessions can do much to strengthen relationships. The more team members initiate communication, the better.

There are times when the supervisor must initiate the process. Intervention by the supervisor is necessary when situations develop that are hurting the operation's productivity. Naturally, private communication is a sensitive procedure. It takes a good sense of timing, a smooth approach, and enough personal confidence to get things started.

Supervisors may avoid giving feedback even when they know that talking to their team members could solve problems and increase their team's productivity. The most common reasons managers fail to have these conversations is a fear of the unknown and the need for sensitivity.

THE ART OF COMMUNICATION

The art of communication is not difficult to master. Use these tips to get started.

1. A quiet voice is more effective and less threatening than a loud voice.

2. A good way to dissipate a team member's hostility is to let him or her talk it out first. Do not interrupt.

3. When the team member is talking (perhaps defending some action), listen instead of planning your rebuttal.

4. Periods of silence can help the team member do some important self-evaluation, so do not rush to break in on him or her.

5. Free and honest communication is restricted when a time limit is imposed or implied.

6. Since most abuse coming from team members is directed at the system, the company, or themselves, do not take negative comments personally.

7. The resolution of a problem is not the only sign of a successful counseling period. The mere act of achieving two-way communication is worthwhile.

8. Attempt to end all sessions on a positive note. Thanking the employee for meeting with you is a good way to accomplish this.

9. Schedule a follow-up meeting.

THE FIVE R'S OF PRIVATE COMMUNICATION

Private communication is a necessary tool in a supervisor's survival kit. It requires no magic; you can start right away without fear or misgivings if you understand and use the following principles. Once you learn these principles—the five R's—private communication will become one of your most important management tools:

1. **Right** purpose,

2. **Right** time,

3. **Right** place,

4. **Right** approach,

5. **Right** techniques.

The Right Purpose

The primary job of the manager is to keep relationships healthy, and private communication is the best tool for this task. It should be used, however, only when the break in the relationship has caused a drop in productivity. Managers *must not* pry into team members' lives.

> With customer count down and labor out for the month, Darlean's manager, Allan, sent her home early twice last week.
>
> This week Darlean's customers have been complaining that her manners are less than "friendly."
>
> Today, Allan approached Darlean and before he could say anything, Darlean angrily told him that she is not the only person on the clock and she was not going to take this abuse anymore.
>
> In talking privately with Darlean, Allan was able to learn that Darlean thought that he was picking on her, and she didn't know he was cutting hours to save on labor costs. More important, Allan learned that Darlean was upset that she didn't make enough money in tips and was worried about paying her electric bill. In talking privately with Darlean, Allan was able to share information, empathize with Darlean's situation, and restore the relationship.

Private communication should be used *only* for the specific purposes presented in the following list:

■ *To motivate team members to achieve greater productivity.* Private communication sometimes can help a new team member bring productivity up to standard or help more experienced team members increase their productivity.

In this example, Ramona shows how private communication worked to motivate one of her team members.

> Joe, who had done an excellent job for four months as a part-time team member, started arriving late, making mistakes, and otherwise interrupting the smooth operation of the kitchen. Ramona moved in with a 15-minute counseling session. She discovered that Joe had been so involved with a personal problem that he had lost sight of his goal, which was to earn enough money to finish college. As a result of the discussion with Ramona, Joe was able to focus on his goal and his part-time job became important again. His productivity was soon back up to its normal level.

■ *To resolve personality conflicts.* Working relationships between two team members in the same department can sometimes deteriorate, causing emotional conflicts and a drop in productivity. In order to protect both the department and other team members, it is sometimes wise for a manager to become involved. The following incident is a case in point.

> Mrs. Singletary made the mistake of badgering Ms. Jones about her productivity. The two ladies work together processing linens for a 400-room hotel. Ms. Jones reacted by sulking and letting her productivity drop below standard. Ms. Jones's manager, Joe, heard the rumble and invited Mrs. Singletary to talk it over. He felt that Mrs. Singletary should take the initiative (with Joe's help) to restore the injured relationship because of her maturity and

ability. The repair work took time and required much outside support from Joe, but this approach worked.

- *To discipline a team member.* Typically the first step in a company's disciplinary procedure is called a "counseling" session. The session is an opportunity to communicate privately with your employee. Use the time to discuss the problem and to explore alternatives for solving it. Skillful counseling is the best possible tool to use in correcting a team member's violation of rules, procedures, or policies. It is a sensitive task to discipline others, but when it must be done, it requires a private setting to ensure that others do not overhear the discussion. Alberta used this technique effectively to correct a bad habit and enable Mr. Spencer to save face.

  > Mr. Spencer was socializing too much with other team members, extending his meal breaks, and making nonbusiness telephone calls to friends and family members. His team leader, Alberta, was inclined to be tolerant until she noticed that his activities were affecting the productivity of others. She invited Mr. Spencer into what became a 20-minute counseling session. Alberta stated her concerns quickly but was careful not to show any hostility. She also gave Mr. Spencer a chance to defend some of his actions. The period ended with a positive exchange by both parties. After two weeks, Alberta was pleased with the way Mr. Spencer had curtailed his socializing.

- *To terminate a team member.* Terminating an employee is never easy, but when handled properly, it can substantially help the team member, the manager, and the company.

  > Due to a cutback in staff, Larry was forced to terminate a team member some months ago. Rather than handle it in a cold, one-way manner, Larry took the time to discuss the situation at length with the team member in a counseling environment. He also provided the individual with a good reference as well as other assistance. The team member left the company in a better frame of mind, and, of course, Larry felt better too.

(Companies are subject to federal Equal Employment Opportunity Commission [EEOC] laws and should adopt a disciplinary procedure. In cases where the company is accused of wrongful discharge or discrimination, the courts review the disciplinary procedure; the company that doesn't have such a procedure is flirting with a lawsuit.)

- *To conduct orientation.* Orienting new team members is an excellent time to engage in private communication. Many supervisors set up a formal orientation period with new team members during the first day on the job, at the end of the first week, and at the end of the first month to help them adjust and successfully make it through the probationary period. It is imperative that the supervisor orients all new team members. Turnover rates, job-related accidents, and job satisfaction are strongly correlated to whether or not an employee receives an orientation. The better the orientation, the higher the satisfaction and the lower turnover and accidents will be. The manager should not delegate orientation to another team member nor assume that the company's human resources department has done the job. The manager is accountable for introducing new team members to co-workers, showing them around, and covering policies such breakrooms and break times, starting and quitting times, and paydays. Company policies and procedures that directly affect the new team member's work also should be thoroughly covered during orientation. The manager should prepare an orientation manual containing pertinent information, frequently asked questions, and important phone numbers. The new team member can then refer to it as needed.

The Right Time

Timing (usually under the control of the supervisor) is very important to a successful outcome. If the timing is right, the results can be excellent. If the timing is wrong, little may be accomplished.

Here are four suggestions that should help you choose the right time.

1. **Do not intervene until you are sure it is necessary.** An isolated or first-time event is not a pattern. Every team member has a few bad days or a temporary struggle with his or her attitude. Use private communication only after a team member's productivity has shown a downward trend over a period of time. You do not want to jump in too early or, conversely, allow too much time to elapse before confronting the situation. Remember, however, that premature intervention can do more harm than good.

2. **Do not initiate private communication when you yourself are upset, frustrated, or angry.** Counseling is a two-way affair, and if you use that opportunity to get rid of some inner hostility, it will kill any chance of a successful session.

3. **Remember that certain times of the day are not appropriate.** Peak activity periods, just before lunch and at the end of the day (when team members may be anxious to get home or meet appointments), are not the most suitable times to talk with employees. Also, try to avoid periods when the team member may be upset emotionally, unless the cause of the upset is the reason for the intervention.

4. **Do not set up a private communication session too far in advance.** If you invite a team member to meet you in your office at 2:00 P.M. when it is only 10:00 A.M., he or she has four hours to worry and get upset. In almost all cases, it is better to set a time with either a short gap or none at all.

The Right Place

Having the right place for private communication can be more important than you think. It is almost impossible to have a successful conversation in a noisy place with frequent distractions. The ideal situation, of course, is a private office. Some supervisors must settle for less. One solution is to use coffee break time, provided that outsiders do not interfere. Another alternative is to make arrangements to use somebody else's office or a vacant room.

The Right Approach

The major reason managers back away from this type of problem solving is that they are afraid of the first hurdle, the approach. They think about it and plan it, but not knowing how to take the first step prevents them from executing their plans. At least four primary fears cause this hesitation:

1. fear of saying the wrong thing at the beginning, thereby causing an unpleasant confrontation,

2. fear of invading the team member's privacy,

3. fear of opening up a hornet's nest of other problems, and

4. fear of being disliked by the team member.

Most of these fears are not substantiated by fact. Team members like to talk to their leaders, even about unpleasant matters. They do not always resent being disciplined, if it is done in the right way, and often admit that help was needed, even though they would not ask for it.

To get past these fears, managers need a formula or procedure to follow. The following procedure is suggested if you have a difficult problem to face.

1. Invite the person into your office or other designated place, without advance notice. This eliminates time for fear to build, which can create a threatening climate.

2. Start the conversation quickly and do not beat around the bush. Try saying something like this: "We have something important to talk about; we will both benefit if we get to it."

3. Only state the facts. Do not make accusations. Try to keep a calm, pleasant, subdued voice and encourage the team member to talk. Do not rush.

4. Pay attention to the talk : listen ratio. Often it is better to do more listening than talking.

As you develop your own formula, one that fits your personality, you will find that it is not difficult to launch even a potentially unpleasant session.

The Right Technique

The two basic techniques used for private communication are directive and nondirective. Using the directive technique, the supervisor does most of the talking and determines the direction the interview will take. The supervisor should use this approach in a gentle and quiet manner, however, because constructive private communication ends when an argument begins. The team member should sense that advice or direction is being given to help him or her.

The directive type is considered appropriate for the following situations:

- when a violation of company rules or policies has occurred,
- when a serious lack of performance needs to be corrected, or

■ when a team member's hostility (toward you, others, or the company) has reached a stage where it can no longer be tolerated.

The nondirective type is quite different. The supervisor does less talking and encourages the team member to communicate more. It is a soft approach designed to bring hidden problems out into the open or to set a climate for free and constructive discussion on any matter important to the team member. This permissive, unstructured type of communication is often therapeutic and provides motivation for the team member. It is the only technique to use when no problem exists; it is considered the best approach for the following situations:

■ when a team member appears to have lost her or his positive attitude over a sustained period of time, resulting in lower productivity,

■ when you want to strengthen or restore a relationship, or

■ when you feel you can motivate a team member to achieve greater productivity.

CONCLUSION

Effective communication is a required skill for effective leadership. Your communication skills may be called on for a variety of important reasons. Supervisors are often called on to counsel with employees on work-related performance issues. In cases where the employee requires formal disciplinary action, counseling is required in most disciplinary procedures. In many procedures the first stage, or step one, is called a "counseling" session.

An employee may initiate a private conversation with his or her supervisor about matters of a personal nature and not work related. The supervisor may be asked to provide a listening ear. When this occurs it is best to remember that you are not a trained counselor so don't "play doctor." That is, do not diagnose symptoms or prescribe treatment. Often a good listener is all that is needed to help. In serious cases the supervisor may suggest that the employee seek out resources available in the company such as an EAP (employee assistance program). Many companies provide this resource. If one is not available through their employer, employees may be advised to seek out social service agencies within the community especially for personal problems that are outside the workplace.

Effective communications builds strong relationships. Remember that how well you communicate will define the quality of your relationships with others. Effective communication cannot solve problems alone. It can, however, be the important first step.

DISCUSSION QUESTIONS

1. What additional reasons might explain why supervisors are reluctant to initiate private communication sessions with their team members? What would you suggest to a manager who has this problem?

2. Some people claim that young supervisors today find it more difficult to participate in private communication sessions, especially for discipline or termination, than their older counterparts. Do you agree or disagree? Why?

3. Does frequent informal communication between a supervisor and a team member eliminate the need for private communication? Build your case one way or the other.

4. How would a supervisor have a private conversation with a team member regarding the following?
   a. outstanding job performance
   b. perfect attendance
   c. promotional opportunities
   d. inappropriate uniform
   e. offensive body odor
   f. tardiness
   g. drop in productivity
   h. violating a safety or other company rule
   i. personal non–work-related issue

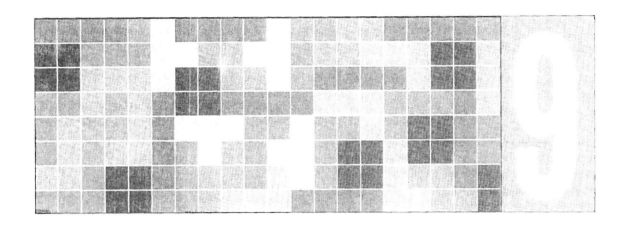

Solving Performance Problems

After you have finished reading this chapter, you should be able to

- describe the skills needed to deal confidently with problem team members,

- define the different circumstances that would call for a corrective conference and a noncorrective conference,

- suggest ways to overcome hostilities in the workplace, and

- describe how to address problems professionally, not personally.

ADDRESSING THE PROBLEM TEAM MEMBER

A problem team member will affect a good team member. The good team member may quit or create new problems. At some point you will encounter a team member who will purposefully challenge your tolerance, ignore your guidance, and violate written rules or policies. When this happens, you may either abandon your role as a leader or define it. This chapter will help you address with confidence one of the hardest components of your job—dealing with troubling behavior.

A problem team member is one who repeatedly violates a departmental rule or policy, frequently causes disturbances among other team members, or lowers productivity through some form of unacceptable behavior. Eventually, every supervisor must deal with such a team member. Problem members can quickly destroy the effectiveness of a team. Managers and team leaders do not have the luxury of letting time take care of such individuals and cannot sweep the problem under the carpet.

Your image as a supervisor is important. Keep in mind that other team members will be watching how you respond to the problem employee on your staff more closely than management; studies show that most co-workers have a lower tolerance for problem team members than managers expect. Your team members want you to solve the issue to make life easier for them. When employees become problems, the rest of the team expects you do to your job.

The techniques for private communication covered in the previous chapter will come to your rescue in these situations. A skillful supervisor is often able to turn a problem team member into a superior team member by discovering the cause of the problem and coming up with a workable solution during a counseling session. In some cases, however, the only acceptable solution is to take disciplinary action, which may end with the dismissal of the team member. Every case deserves individual analysis and treatment.

Diane, a single parent, was demonstrating an increasing amount of hostility toward her fellow team members and customers—so much so that other cashiers were reluctant to work with her because she acted so hostile. Customers complained that she wasn't friendly, and yesterday a party of six left after being rudely greeted by her at the door. After two counseling sessions, Diane's problems were narrowed down to an imbalance between home and career. Diana was feeling the stress of parenthood compounded by a schedule that conflicted with the availability of her babysitter. Diane was unable to separate the two and, as a result, she was adding home problems to job demands. Diane needed a schedule that was different than her current one. Her behavior irritated co-workers, created customer complaints, and put unreasonable demands on her supervisor. Once the situation was isolated and discussed, Diane's supervisor counseled her on her behavior, shared with her the need to mend relations with other team members, and cautioned her about her treatment of customers. Diane's schedule was changed and Diane was encouraged to bring challenges to her supervisor's attention before it became a problem in performance. Diane was able to discipline herself to achieve a better home–career balance, and she was no longer a problem team member.

Chris was a classic example of how frustration can create a problem team member. A recent graduate from a hotel management program, Chris had set excessively high career goals for himself. As a result, he became frustrated over his slow progress; this frustration, in turn, resulted in aggressive behavior. For example, Chris would lose his patience in working with others and walk away in a huff. During staff meetings, he would seek controversy and vent his feelings. After two counseling sessions, Chris recognized his own problem and found employment in a new environment where his talents and education could be put to more immediate use.

FACING DISAGREEMENT OR CONFLICT

As a supervisor, you may run into a conflict with a team member, a peer, or your own boss. Four steps will help guide you through such an experience so that the best solution is found and both you and the other party maintain a healthy relationship.

1. **Don't put the other person down.** It is important to preserve the integrity and self-respect of all parties. In a heated discussion, it is easy to say something demeaning. To avoid this trap, keep your focus on the issue, not the person.

2. **Search for common ground.** Try to see things from the other person's perspective so that you can compromise and find a way to resolve the matter. To better understand the other person's position, you must listen with empathy and be flexible.

3. **Do not expect behavioral changes.** The purpose of resolving conflicts is to find agreement on what must be done, not whether a behavioral change is required of you or the other party.

4. **Compromise is not throwing in the towel.** The goal is to find the best solution to improve productivity and reach agreed-upon goals, not to discover who might be right or wrong. A compromise—especially after an open discussion—can be the best solution for both parties and the company.

Agreeing to a compromise does not mean you have given up your individuality. It simply means you understand that a conflict exists and that you are willing to help resolve it.

It's Professional, Not Personal

There is no doubt that emotions can run high when situations occur that challenge your authority. You may take it personally when team members pull against you or against the goals of your department. Maybe it is personal for the team member. Maybe his or her behavior is intentional. Maybe he or she is trying to incite you to behave unprofessionally. Under no circumstance can you allow this to happen. You should never lose your professionalism. Never allow your reactions to become a problem.

Leaders who forsake their professionalism compromise their ability to act with due diligence.

■ *Stand up for your principles.* Either performance is right or it is wrong. Either way, you are required to respond to it.

Leaders who forsake their professionalism sacrifice their authority and are stripped of their respect.

■ *Use common sense.* Team members know the different between right and wrong. They choose their behavior. Your job is to observe and respond to performance—right or wrong.

Leaders who forsake their professionalism set themselves up for failure by showing other team members they are incapable of handling challenges that test their position.

■ *Enforce polices.* Compliance and enforcement of company polices and guidelines are not an option; they are a requirement.

Leaders who forsake their professionalism often find themselves facing disciplinary action themselves.

■ *Clarify expectations.* Expectations change for various reasons. Be sure that your followers know your expectations and are trained to meet them.

These are the emotional anchors that will keep you emotionally grounded.

Keep in mind the following five fundamentals so that you view the team member, and the problems he or she is creating, with a professional perspective.

1. **Remain optimistic.** Have faith in your ability to resolve the problem and to build a better relationship with the individual. You must initiate communication with the team member if the problem is to be dealt with openly and a solution reached. If you fear the process, you are already at a disadvantage.

2. **Open up communications.** Accept the premise that you can find a solution that is best for the individual, you, and the company. You can find a solution through open, two-way communication. Your goal is to save the team member, keep him or her in your department, and convert the individual into a productive member of your team. The more you anticipate good results, the more likely they are to occur.

3. **Avoid becoming defensive.** Recognize that severe discipline at the beginning often intensifies an existing problem. Both you and the team member may have a tendency to be defensive. If you create a threatening climate, the team member may become emotional. The problem team member can

become more of a problem and a solution becomes impossible. Another reason a heavy hand at the beginning can backfire is that severe discipline can cause other team members to feel uncomfortable.

4. **Control your timing.** The longer you wait to correct unacceptable behavior, the more explosive the conference may become. Most supervisors who delay taking action permit the behavior of the problem team member to get under their skin, where it festers until the supervisor can no longer deal with it objectively. The sooner you deal with a problem, the less emotional you will be.

> Jason tolerated Rosemary's disruptive behavior for six weeks without saying a word. Each time she violated his line of discipline, his dislike for her increased. Each time she was insensitive to customers and co-workers, he became more frustrated. Finally, one morning he reached his tolerance level, invited her into his office, and exploded. The moment the conference was over, Jason knew he had made several mistakes. His relationship with Rosemary had worsened, and he could not see any chance to restore it in the future. He had a guilty feeling about his behavior, and he knew it had hurt his relationships with her co-workers. He was ineffective for the rest of the day. As a result, Jason resolved to deal with such problems as soon as they surfaced in the future.

5. **Protect yourself and your organization.** Accept the fact that a single problem team member can cause your downfall as a supervisor.

> Some co-workers did not think that Francine was ready for her promotion to training director of the Eggs with Bacon restaurant chain, but management thought differently, and their confidence in her seemed justified, at least during the first months. A serious cloud appeared when Shirlean, a trainer, became a problem. It started when Shirlean violated the acceptable dress code; it intensified when she became sullen with some server trainees. It became intolerable when it affected the productivity of others. Although Francine had no experience in handling such a situation, she knew she had only three alternatives.
>
> 1. She could delay action.
> 2. She could go to her boss.
> 3. She could initiate a private counseling session today.
>
> Francine decided on the last alternative and immediately called Shirlean into her office. Francine was careful not to create a threatening climate. She did not overplay her hand, but she quickly led into the problem and made it clear that she was in charge and was going to stand her ground. Although she experienced some difficult moments, eventually some healthy two-way communications took place. Shirlean decided that the work environment in the training department was not for her, and one week later she resigned. Shirlean departed without hostility, and Francine had solved her problem. From that moment on, all of her team members seemed to respect her more and productivity increased. Best of all, management was most complimentary. Her immediate supervisor said, "We were monitoring the situation carefully and sensed that your future depended upon how you handled Shirlean. We are extremely pleased."

Keep in mind that you are important to your organization. Do not let a problem team member destroy you. You must deal with the problem team member in legal ways so that both you and the organization are protected. If you need backup assistance, do not hesitate to ask for advice and support from your supervisors. As a beginning supervisor, you are not supposed to know all the answers, so do not let personal pride keep you from seeking support. In dealing with problem team members, it can be a serious mistake to act prematurely on your own.

Even if you accept these fundamentals and practice them, solving team member problems will not be easy. Many, however, are less difficult than they appear. For example, a team member may become a problem in your eyes but not in the eyes of others. The team member may be irritating you but not co-workers or other management personnel.

> Roger had a solid reputation as a superior supervisor, but he became irritated with Tony, a management trainee, the first day Tony was assigned to his department. Roger thought Tony was too aggressive. He immediately disciplined Tony in an unfair, unprofessional way, which is not his usual attitude. Then, by chance, he overheard two of his regular team members defending Tony. Roger took stock of himself, admitted he had been unfair, and made a complete turnaround. As a result, he built an excellent relationship with Tony. What he had interpreted as aggressiveness was assertiveness that others appreciated.

Your discipline, or authority line, is essential so team members respect you and maintain a high level of productivity. Discipline must be maintained at all costs. But the supervisor must be careful to treat all team members fairly and consistently. Maintaining productivity leaves no room for personal vendettas between a supervisor and a team member.

The supervisor must protect his or her discipline line in quiet, effective ways or eventually lose the respect of those on the team. To permit one team member to cross the line is to lose the respect of those who still honor it. When the supervisor loses authority, productivity and morale can drop drastically.

> Joel had been able to maintain a relaxed, comfortable line of discipline for almost six months. Not a single team member was taking advantage of him. Then Victoria, who was having personal problems, started testing the line from all directions. She not only challenged traditional procedures she had previously honored, but she started to make complaints to Joel's boss. The conflict came to a head when she challenged Joel openly on a procedural matter in a staff meeting.
>
> Joel initiated a long conference the following day to discuss her recent behavior in relationship to departmental productivity. The atmosphere was tense until near the end of the conference. The conversation turned to Victoria's career goal at this point and Joel stated that he would like to help her reach it. Eventually a kind of trade-off took place: Victoria promised to be more sensitive to Joel and departmental objectives, and Joel agreed to do what he could to prepare her for her career goal without favoring her over others. Their civility contract lasted until Victoria earned a promotion six months later.

CORRECTIVE CONFERENCES AND DISCIPLINARY PROCEDURES

Most federal and state employment laws are enforced on companies that employ 50 or more employees. Having a disciplinary procedure in place will help the supervisor avoid expensive litigation. The disciplinary procedure must be consistently and fairly imposed on all employees. Most disciplinary procedures get more punitive at each step, ending in termination for those cases taken to the extreme. For this reason, employment laws require that all employees be given due process when punishment is forthcoming. Due process is a right. Protecting and providing due process is a primacy reason to have a procedure. If you do not follow an adopted procedure that protects this right, you may face expensive legal action, pay unemployment compensation for wrongful termination, or both.

Changing inappropriate behavior to appropriate behavior is the primary purpose of the disciplinary procedure. A typical procedure does this through a timed, sequenced series of steps that become more punitive in nature as the steps progress toward the final stage, termination. The effective supervisor knows the procedure inside and out and uses it when necessary.

A Typical Disciplinary Procedure

Most organizations differentiate rules violations according to severity and nature. Violations such as being late for work, making mistakes, and absenteeism are considered minor and are usually dealt with using the disciplinary procedure. Serious offenses, such as fighting, stealing, or drug-related activities, are grounds for immediate termination. Documentation is needed regardless of the offense and is kept in the employee's file for a predetermined length of time.

The following is an outline of a typical disciplinary procedure for violations of minor company rules and policies that do not warrant immediate termination. A thorough explanation of each stage is provided.

Stage 1: Exploratory or counseling conference

Stage 2: Corrective conference 1

Stage 3: Corrective conference 2

Stage 4: Notice of termination

Stage 1: The Exploratory or Counseling Conference

The purpose of the exploratory conference is to lay the problem on the table in a nonthreatening manner. Both parties should have an equal chance to communicate; both old and new facts should be introduced and, if possible, the roots of the problem should be revealed. Sometimes the exploratory conference can do it all.

> Sally took Jennifer out to lunch to discover what was causing Jennifer's hostility. She found a private place, made certain that the environment was relaxed, and introduced the subject. The discussion that followed showed that Jennifer thought Sally had been unfair to her and that her resentment had created a barrier between them. As a result, she had violated the departmental discipline line to show her independence. When Sally convinced Jennifer that the unfair treatment had not been intended, they both agreed to start from scratch. The exploratory conference had solved the problem. No further action was necessary.
>
> Cyrus, the General Manager, received two Hidden Shoppers' reports that Constance, the sanitation worker, had violated safety regulations by not posting wet floor signs near the area she was mopping. He called her into his office and

quickly introduced the subject. It turned out that Constance was uninformed about the safety regulations and had not been aware that she was breaking them. When he received no further reports, Cyrus figured the exploratory conference had corrected the problem.

If a team member's behavior is not appropriate, the reason may be caused by inadequate training. Be sure to check to see whether the team member knows how to perform his or her job duties correctly before taking disciplinary action.

Stage 2: Corrective Conference 1

When the exploratory conference tells the supervisor that the problem is perpetual, a follow-up session is necessary. Such a follow-up can take one of two forms. In cases that show evidence that firm rules have been broken, the supervisor initiates a series of corrective conferences. In cases where the human relations problems are complex, one or more noncorrective follow-up discussions may be necessary to resolve the problem. The decision to conduct follow-up conferences can be made during the exploratory conference or later. Each case requires individual analysis. Sometimes the exploratory conference is interpreted as a warning by the problem team member; sometimes it is not.

Assume that during an exploratory conference you suspect that a problem team member is violating a rule, but you have no evidence. Later, however, you collect the evidence. At that point you set up Corrective Conference 1. This conference is, in effect, a documented warning.

The purpose of this first conference is to verify that the violation occurred and warn the team member by reviewing documentation of the violation. Although required documentation varies among organizations, it should include

- a specific description of the violation,

- the name of the violator,

- the date the incident occurred,

- the date of the corrective conference, and

- the written acknowledgment or rebuttal of the team member.

If the problem is corrected, be sure your employee knows how much you appreciate his or her cooperation.

Stage 3: Corrective Conference 2

This conference does not need to take place unless a further violation is reported. If a second incident (even a different violation) is reported, the second conference should take place with the same documentation procedure. This meeting becomes a second warning. There may be some form of punitive action taken against the employee, such as a suspension without pay.

Stage 4: Notice of Termination

This conference is necessary only if a third violation occurs. The procedure will vary according to each organization (and the operation's legal counsel), but generally it will include

- a third person (another manager, a upper management person, a representative from the human resource department, or staff lawyer),

- a review and presentation of previous documented warnings, and

- notice of termination.

Whatever the procedure, the supervisor should permit two-way communication and attempt to show the team member that he or she has been treated fairly. The rights of the team member must be protected at all costs.

When this procedure is followed carefully, most team members will improve their performance or submit their resignation voluntarily before Corrective Conference 2 takes place before termination.

Follow-Up Conferences

Assume that during an exploratory conference you discover a deep-seated human relations problem. Perhaps a personality conflict between two co-workers is damaging productivity. Maybe one team member's attitude is so negative that it is hurting the productivity of others or causing customer complaints. Possibly a conflict has arisen between you and the problem team member. Situations of this nature call for one or two follow-up conferences.

A single exploratory conference will not solve most human relations problems. It takes time to dissipate misunderstandings and misinterpretations. When an exploratory conference reveals hostility between the supervisor and a team member, for example, the conflict may never be solved. Holding one or two follow-up conferences, however, is more effective than trying once and giving up.

> Jane was disturbed to discover that Carol was upset and hostile toward her. About all she was able to accomplish during the exploratory conference was to listen and let Carol get her inner anxieties and frustrations out in the open. Three days later Jane conducted a follow-up conference with more of a two-way discussion that was less volatile. At this stage, both individuals admitted to some mistakes and misinterpretations. The relationship was beginning to be rebuilt. Later Jane initiated a third conference in which mutual rewards were discussed. Eventually the relationship was fully restored, and all hostility dissipated.

As this example illustrates, more than one follow-up conference is often necessary to solve a human relations problem. The process of restoration is not easy or fast. In most cases, some give-and-take is necessary to build a new foundation for mutual respect, and some behavioral changes must take place on both sides between conferences. The supervisor should not expect to be able to solve all human problems, but in most cases the combination of good exploratory techniques and one or more follow-up conferences is an excellent way to ensure harmony and high productivity in a department.

Give the conference process a chance to work. Inexperienced managers sometimes become discouraged if they do not see immediate results. Resolving conflicts, helping others change their attitudes, and dissipating hostility takes time. Remind yourself that although the process does not always work, it works often enough to be worth your effort. Even if you fail, you will have the satisfaction of having tried.

WHEN THE TEAM MEMBER IS UNABLE TO REACH STANDARDS

You may have to learn to live with certain low-level team members. One or more team members in your department may never live up to your expectations. These individuals do not lower the productivity of others or cross your discipline line, but they contribute less than other workers do. For example, you may have a mature team member who has seniority but cannot adjust quickly to dramatic changes or a team member who refuses to communicate but produces better than average work. Such team members can make your job as a supervisor more difficult, but they are not troublemakers.

Sometimes counseling will strengthen these team members; sometimes it will not. When you have done your best to change their behavior, you must continue to be positive with these team members without letting them pull you down or hurt your leadership ability.

WHEN CHEMICAL DEPENDENCY IS INVOLVED

To maintain and increase productivity, supervisors need to be alert to the possibility of chemical dependency (including alcohol abuse) among team members. Tolerating abuse/addiction is not in the best interest of the team member, the supervisor, or the organization. Most companies have a zero tolerance approach to chemical abuse. Check with your human resource department for your company's policy.
How do you handle suspected dependency problems?

- Know your organization's policy and conform to it.

- Recognize that a problem exists.

- Always consult your superior before you begin any form of intervention.

- Have a third person present should a discussion with the team member take place.

As a supervisor, you are the key person in terms of monitoring job performance. It is up to you to provide documentation of failure to reach standards. Should such documentation show a possible dependency problem, it is time to consult a superior and bring in a professional. Procrastination is not the answer.

WHEN SEXUAL HARASSMENT OCCURS

Sexual harassment is behavior of a sexual nature on the part of one person that causes another person to be uncomfortable. In most cases, sexual harassment is more than a single incident; it is a deliberate pattern of behavior pursued over a period of time.

Sexual harassment violates the law and inhibits work performance. Victims can be male or female, a manager or subordinate, or a vendor or customer. It is the responsibility of the supervisor or team leader to create and maintain a working environment where no form of harassment from any source is permitted.

The following steps are recommended to create a work environment free of sexual harassment:

1. The topic of harassment should be discussed openly in a staff meeting, and the supervisor should state the legal parameters and encourage complaints from any individual.

2. Upon receiving a complaint, the supervisor should listen and record the specific conditions under which the alleged harassment took place.

3. The supervisor should then take up the matter with the director of human resources or another superior for verification and possible action.

4. In counseling an individual who may be guilty of sexual harassment, the supervisor is advised to have a third-party specialist present.

5. The individual who initiated the complaint should be advised on the action taken and encouraged to return should any further harassment occur.

CONCLUSION

A problem team member is one who repeatedly violates a departmental rule or policy, frequently causes disturbances among other team members, or lowers productivity through some form of unacceptable behavior. Agreeing to a compromise does not mean you have given up your individuality. Do not let a problem team member destroy you. You must deal with the problem team member in legal ways so that both you and the organization are protected. Federal and state employment laws affect all organizations with 50 or more employees. Supervisors must use an established disciplinary procedure. To maintain and increase productivity, supervisors need to be alert to the possibility of chemical dependency (including alcohol abuse) among team members. Sexual harassment violates the law and inhibits work performance.

DISCUSSION QUESTIONS

1. How can a problem team member affect
   a. other team members?
   b. your career?

2. Assuming that the supervisor is a skillful communicator, what are the chances a problem team member will improve after having an exploratory conference with his or her supervisor? Defend your answer.

3. In what specific ways might a new supervisor build sufficient personal confidence to deal with a problem team member on a one-on-one basis?

4. If a problem team member resigns voluntarily between corrective communication sessions 1 and 2, has the procedure failed? Explain your views.

5. How would you ensure a harassment-free workplace?

6. Explain the difference between a supervisor who addresses team members professionally versus a manager who approaches problems personally. Which supervisor is likely to be more successful in his or her career? Why?

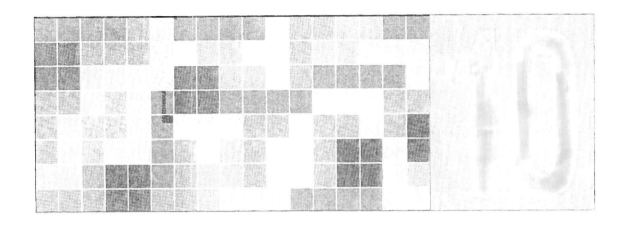

Keeping Turnover
from Being a Problem

After you have finished reading this chapter, you should be able to

■ explain five main reasons team members quit,

■ discuss how to prepare for an interview,

■ describe how to complete orientation of new employees,

■ discuss the role of part-time employees in the hospitality industry, and

■ discuss the art of scheduling.

WHY TEAM MEMBERS QUIT

Every year companies provide every employee (past and present) a W-2 form. Because of turnover, hospitality companies, particularly restaurants, will generate enough W-2 forms to mail to 5 to 10 times the number they currently have on the company payroll.

We don't have problems finding people to hire. We have problems keeping the people we hire. Most team members who quit will quit within the first 30 days of employment. Why? Most likely it will be for one of the following reasons:

1. **Job expectations.** Team members quit because their job expectations are not met. They realize that what they agreed to do when they took the job is not the job they are doing.

   ■ Jamie is a waitress and a single mother. She works during the day so she can be home with her kids at night. For the second week in a row, she is scheduled to work evenings. She has to pay for a babysitter when she works evenings. When she was hired, she told her manager she could work days and every other weekend. When she brought this to her manager's attention, he told her he scheduled her when he needed her the most.

   ■ Sam was told he could train to be a cook in the kitchen. That's hard to do when he is always scheduled in the dishroom.

   ■ Kelly needs to work 40 hours a week to pay his bills. After being sent home early twice this week, he will only work 28 hours.

   ■ Cindy was hired as a hostess to greet guests and direct customer flow. However, she spends most of her time bussing tables. She resents having to wear her nice clothes to bus tables.

   When job expectations do not match actual job conditions, it is realistic to expect dissatisfaction. Left uncorrected, dissatisfaction leads to turnover.

2. **Sense of belonging.** Team members quit because they don't feel welcome. This occurs when

   ■ The team members are new and the veteran team members mock them for being new and inexperienced.

   ■ The new team members are more than capable of doing their jobs, but they are alienated by well-established cliques of other team members in the store. Vindictive cliques will run off new team members.

- The manager fails to build mutual respect and admiration between new team members and veteran team members. This is particularly bad when the manager is relying on the veteran team member to train the new team member. When the veteran team member feels put upon because of the responsibility of training the new team member, the new team member will be treated badly. Most new team members can't or won't subject themselves to this.
- The supervisor ignores, avoids, or ridicules the new team member.
- The new team member doesn't have a friend at work.

3. **Training.** Team members quit because they are not taught to be successful. No one likes to fail. Too often, we hire people and put them to work without the proper orientation and training. Many organizations use the "baptism by fire" method of training. Those frustrated by an unstructured or nonexistent training program won't allow themselves to be burned by the flames too many times.

4. **Opportunities.** Team members quit because they are denied opportunities to grow. Exciting, stimulating work retains employees. Team members thrive on the opportunity to learn new skills, to be promoted, and to be more valuable in their own eyes as well as the eyes of their company. Stagnation, boredom, and the feeling of being confined result in the loss of team members.

5. **Recognition and rewards.** Team members quit because they feel unappreciated; they are not recognized and rewarded for their work. Recognizing and rewarding team members often can be accomplished by saying two simple, powerful words: "thank you." Failing to appreciate team members is the number one reason why team members quit.

TEAM MEMBER TURNOVER

The lower the turnover the better—as long as you are *keeping the right team members*. Not everyone who quits working leaves the organization. Many team members who quit still report to work. They clock in on your time clock and work as little as possible. The results: high labor costs, low productivity, and disgruntled team members. No matter how hard you try to staff your facility, until you start keeping the people who can help you build your business and lose the people that are costing you business, you will never be successful.

Team member stability and high productivity often go together, but frequent personnel turnover is a fact of life in the hospitality industry. No matter how effective you become as a supervisor, now and then a key team member will shock you with a resignation. A promotion or lateral move that is good for your company also can create a problem for the supervisor.

Mary was pleased that management had selected Carla as general manager of the country store. It was a high compliment to Mary, who had trained Carla as her assistant, but the decision would mean screening, employing, and training a replacement. Which of her current staff could best fill Carla's shoes? Would now be a good time to hire from within? How could she turn the vacancy into an advantage?

Personnel changes present major challenges to all supervisors—challenges that must be approached with sound planning and vision.

As a new supervisor, Virginia set out to hire a qualified replacement for a team member who had left. Without any background in interviewing, Virginia selected an individual with a persuasive personality but also with psychological problems. Further investigation would have revealed that the applicant had been a problem team member in all of her previous jobs. Virginia lived with the situation for six months. Finally, after the conflicts that arose rendered Virginia so ineffective that her own job was on the line, the individual was fired after being caught falsifying her timecard. Inexperience had caused Virginia to hire a problem rather than solve one.

Every person you hire will have one of three effects on your staff. Your new hire will either

1. elevate the performance of your staff,

2. lower the performance of your staff, or

3. have no significant impact on the performance of your staff.

As a supervisor, you may or may not become deeply involved in the staffing process. Some supervisors have complete control over who is hired or transferred to their units; others are assigned new team members from the human resource department, with or without refusal power. The more your role as a supervisor involves you in the staffing process, the more skills you must develop in the staffing process.

THE STAFFING PROCESS

Staffing includes much more than simply filling a vacancy. It also involves determination of long-term personnel needs, orientation and training, transfers and reassignments, rotations, performance evaluations, and terminations. Experienced supervisors ask themselves these questions when determining staffing needs:

■ Could the tasks be divided among other team members?

■ Do I have a backup person trained in all my key positions?

■ In what areas do I need additional coverage?

■ Is someone being trained eventually to take my job as supervisor?

■ What kind of new person will contribute to greater productivity?

■ What skills am I missing among the staff?

■ In what skill areas am I weak?

The goal of every supervisor should be to hire, develop, and maintain the most cohesive and productive staff possible. It is not a goal easily reached.

Interviewing

Employment interviews are normally divided into two approaches. One is a guided pattern (directive); the other is less structured or unguided (nondirective). For an inexperienced interviewer, a guided pattern is often best. Although no system is perfect, a guided pattern has the advantage of providing objectivity.

Preparation for the Interview

It is impossible to hire the best available applicant for a given job unless the skills and duties required are known ahead of time. If a printed job description is available, it should be carefully reviewed and brought up to date. If not, the supervisor should write out the competencies required and revise the job description so it is accurate. Only with such data in hand can the best match between applicants and job be achieved. Here are some additional tips for preparing for interviews:

- Federal and state civil rights laws must be upheld in hiring decisions. Sex, race, and age cannot play a part in the selection process; you must seek and hire the best-qualified person for the job. In addition, disabled people should be considered equally by focusing on what they can do and how they can contribute to productivity.

- The practice of first-come-first-hired should be avoided. Just because a person can fog a mirror doesn't mean he or she should be working for you. There is a difference between hiring a person who is capable of helping you now and hiring a person that becomes your next project. A project is a person who should not have been hired, but rather than dismiss him or her and hire the right person, you take on the project of trying to convert this person into something that the individual is not capable of becoming.

- Be prudent when hiring. Troublesome team members are easier to find than to get rid of. A problem or project team member increases stress, lowers productivity, and inflates labor costs. Such hires also draw into question your competencies as a supervisor.

- You cannot find the best applicant without taking the time to discover what the market has to offer. It is better (and less costly) to take your time in finding and hiring the right person than it is to rush and hire the wrong person.

- Establish skill requirements and expectations before hiring and ensure that an appropriate hiring process is followed. To help ensure that you hire the right team member, focus on examining the interviewee's skills.

- Be prepared to communicate expectations to each new hire and hold him or her accountable.

- Take your time. Screening written applications and interviewing should be done studiously. The more you rush the process, the more subjective you become and the more mistakes are made.

■ As an interview approaches, review the competencies you seek in an applicant (a competency is a skill that can be observed or measured); have a list of questions you intend to ask that will tell you about the applicant's prior related experiences; and identify information you need to provide each applicant regarding the organization and the job. Have a pad available for taking notes and ask probing, open-ended questions that cannot be answered with "yes" or "no."

■ Check references. Even if this is a person's first job, every potential team member should be able to provide you a list of references. Someone should be able to attest to the character and behavior of a potential team member. The time you spend checking references will save you headaches later.

Interviewing Techniques

Interviewing a prospective new team member becomes easier with experience. Ask your Human Resources department for guidance in becoming an effective interviewer. If your organization does not have a Human Resources department, you can get valuable information free of charge from your local Equal Employment Opportunity Commission (EEOC) office. EEOC representatives will also answer questions about the hiring process so you will not violate any federal or state employment laws.

Remember that it is much easier to avoid hiring the wrong person than to fire the wrong person once hired. Generally speaking, it is a good idea to follow these additional steps:

1. Put the applicant at ease so that you can get the most realistic view of how the applicant would perform on the job.

2. Shake hands and ask the applicant to sit down. Provide time for the applicant to answer questions; his or her answers can help you assess the applicant's ability to contribute to your department.

3. Provide the applicant with an opportunity to ask questions.

4. Verify the data on the application form, especially those items pertaining to training and skills.

5. Share accurate information about the position, such as your expectations and the work schedule, that may affect their decision to accept a job if one is offered.

Make a Good First Impression

It is very important for your organization to make a good first impression. You do not want to lose desirable candidates by appearing rude or unsociable. Often, a positive first impression will influence a decision to accept an offer of employment. The following chart provides some tips on how you can make a good first impression.

RELAXING THE APPLICANT

- Welcome the applicant with a smile.
- Shake hands.
- Conduct the interview in a location where you will not be disturbed.
- Offer a beverage such as tea or coffee.
- Engage in light conversation (e.g., the weather, sports, traffic).
- Share information about yourself (e.g., your history, what you enjoy).
- Talk about the opportunities and benefits of the workplace.
- Talk about the position you have available and your expectations.
- Smile.

Interview Questions

Here are some typical questions that interviewers often ask job seekers. These questions are designed to generate a dialogue so that a decision can be based on as much information as possible.

- Why do you want to work here?
- What are your skills in relationship to this position?
- What can you contribute? Why should we hire you?
- Why did you leave your last job? What did you like/dislike about your previous or present job/employer?
- Do you have any weaknesses?
- Is there any thing that would interfere with your doing the tasks expected in the position?
- Tell me about yourself.
- Tell me about a time when you had to
  - ❏ solve a problem quickly
  - ❏ help another co-worker
  - ❏ learn a new skill
  - ❏ help a customer
  - ❏ make a decision in the absence of supervision
  - ❏ deliver bad news
  - ❏ make an unexpected change
  - ❏ meet a deadline
  - ❏ organize an event
  - ❏ resolve a conflict with your supervisor

Questions *not* to Ask

Care should be taken to ask the same questions of all applicants so that comparisons can be made between applicants. Questions of a highly personal nature or those that will embarrass or confuse the applicant should not be used. Do not ask questions that are not job related or are discriminatory in nature. Here are examples of questions you should <u>not</u> ask:

Are you married or do you intend to marry?

Do you have children and, if so, who takes care of them while you work?

Do you go to church, or what is your religious affiliation?

Are you pregnant or do you plan to be pregnant in the near future?

What is your ethnic background?

For a complete list of questions you should not ask, contact your local EEOC office or Human Resources department and request this information. EEOC material is free of charge and extremely helpful.

Ending the Interview

It is important to terminate the interview in a friendly manner without making a false commitment. A suitable closing comment might be, "We will make a decision this Friday. If you do not hear from us by next Monday, we have filled the position with another applicant. We appreciate your interest in our organization, and if you are not offered the position, we will keep your application on file." Even under ideal circumstances, a final choice is difficult to make. It is usually advisable to talk to another supervisor or team leader, especially if two or more candidates appear to be equally qualified.

It is strongly advisable to allow another supervisor or team leader to interview the applicant as well. Having a second opinion of a new hire increases the chances of hiring someone who can benefit the team. It also spurs acceptance of the newly hired team members among veteran team members when they have some say in the process.

Using the Probationary Period

Most organizations have a probationary period that lasts from 30 to 90 days. The probationary period should be used wisely. Use this time to evaluate the performance and overall work-related behaviors of the new hire. If a problem arises, be sure to move in quickly to assess the problem. When behavioral or attitudinal problems surface, it often best to fire the employee rather than allowing him or her to become a permanent team member.

Claude has the most productive unit in the hotel by all measures. This is mainly due to the fact that Claude's staff consists of highly motivated, well-trained employees whose attitudes toward their work and organization are exemplary. Claude explains the reason for this. He does not hire the wrong people. And if by chance he does, he uses the probationary period to weed out those who do not measure up to the high standards of his team. Along with his close observance, his team members are used in the assessment of new hires. They will tell Claude when a problem arises with a probationary employee and are pleased when a nonproductive new hire is not kept on their team. A nonproductive team member means more work for everybody.

Claude knows that most people cannot fake being a responsible, motivated employee for long and uses the probationary period to his advantage.

Orientation and Training

All of the time and energy devoted to finding the best available candidate can go down the drain if the newcomer is not made a full member of the team. The following suggestions are helpful:

- Make sure the new hire is oriented for her or his particular work area. Orientation should be done by the supervisor and not delegated to anyone else.

- See that the new member is introduced to all members of the staff.

- Go over the use of any equipment the new team member will operate.

- Assign a regular team member as a mentor to answer questions and help the new person adjust.

- Make sure that basic department rules and company policies are understood.

- List and discuss specific responsibilities.

- Follow up at the end of the first day or shift to see whether the new team member has questions or whether any adjustments need to be made.

- Studies have shown that poor orientation leads to higher turnover rates and, worse, to accidents. Some supervisors prefer to create and follow an orientation checklist.

A supervisor should monitor the progress of a new team member until he or she has become a relaxed, full partner in the team and is making satisfactory progress toward maximum productivity. If additional training or counseling is required to reach this goal, it should be done quickly. With help, most new team members can make a complete adjustment within one week.

STAFFING ISSUES

Shifting and Rotation

Moving staff members into different roles for both training and motivational purposes is an excellent practice and can measurably improve departmental productivity. Sometimes the employment of a new staff member precipitates such action. Even without turnover, rotating team members from job to job is a good idea in many work environments. Team members who are allowed to stay in the same job too long often fall into a low productivity rut. When given a new challenge, their attitudes improve and they make a bigger contribution. Frequently a simple job exchange can help both team members because the more experience one obtains, the better prepared one becomes for future advancements—including that of supervision. In rotating or shifting team members, the following rules may apply:

1. Discuss proposed changes ahead of time with all parties involved. Allow those affected by the change to be involved in planning the change.

2. Avoid forcing new assignments, especially if the individual is insecure about having the ability to perform in the proposed role.

3. If necessary, provide additional training.

4. Avoid changes unless they are beneficial to both team members and the department as a whole. Expect some drop in productivity until the change is fully adopted.

5. Compliment those who make adjustments gracefully.

Advanced planning accompanied by personal counseling is the key to staff shifting and rotation. Spur-of-the-moment decisions often do more harm than good.

Transfers

When a supervisor senses that he or she has a problem team member, the first thing that often happens is the supervisor transfers the person to another unit. In exceptional cases, such as an irreconcilable conflict between a supervisor and a team member, an in-house transfer may be feasible. Perhaps it will give the individual a new, fresh opportunity; perhaps he or she will be happier under a different management style. However, to initiate a transfer as a ploy to get rid of a problem team member who you know will give the next supervisor a similar problem is not professional. If the request comes from a nonproblem team member, it is another matter. It is possible, for example, that sometime in the future a team member of yours will ask for a transfer so that he or she will be free from your style of supervision. If it happens, do not take it personally. You cannot be expected to have the kind of style that will please everyone. In such cases, a transfer might be advantageous to all the parties involved.

Justifying a Larger Staff

You will hear certain supervisors complaining about their workloads.

- "There is no way to catch up around here."
- "The more we do, the more they pile it on."
- "Too much work—too few people."

Sometimes such complaints are justified. Often they are not. A supervisor should take an overload problem to his or her superior only when all team members and the supervisor are working close to their productivity potentials and the workload continues to increase. In doing so, the following suggestions are made:

1. Demonstrate your overload position with facts. Quote comparative labor cost figures with a similar operation.

2. Compare today's heavier workload with that of past periods in an objective manner.

3. If you cannot justify hiring a full-time team member, consider hiring someone part time.

Whenever a supervisor seeks to increase her or his staff, management will automatically pry into the operation with a sharp eye. Only when such scrutiny produces a well-run department is such a request given serious consideration.

Part-Time Staff

Federal legislation defines a part-time employee as a person who works less than 1000 hours per year (17½ hours per week). Organizations generally view a part-timer as an individual who works 29 hours per week or less. In reality, part-timers work on average about 20 hours a week. Part-time jobs normally have these characteristics:

- Wages and/or hours worked are typically lower than full-time jobs.

- Only the basic or required benefits are provided.

- Some organizations use part-timers as a pool from which to select full-timers.

- Part-time jobs usually offer less job security.

- Part-timers give many types of organizations flexibility and lower labor costs.

Popularity of Part-Time Staff

Some experts claim that full-time, core team members are paid for eight hours of work but actually work closer to six or seven. This discrepancy is because it may take 10 minutes or more for them to get ready to work, two 15-minute breaks are required for 8-hour shifts, and often team members start getting ready to leave before the end of their workday. In contrast, part-time workers employed for four hours a shift may actually work at top performance for almost the entire period.

Part-time workers generally can be divided into three classifications:

1. full-time students who seek "peak period" jobs for approximately 20 hours per week to help with educational expenses,

2. wives and husbands who seek part-time work so they can devote more time to children, and

3. retired people who wish to supplement their retirement incomes.

Many managers claim that part-timers are a welcome challenge when it comes to weaving them into the general mix of team members. They like the enthusiasm, energy, and flexibility part-time workers bring with them. Others claim that the high turnover rate of part-timers negates their advantages.

All agree that it takes additional time and energy from the supervisor to convert part-timers into productive members of a work team.

SUPERVISOR'S RELATIONSHIP WITH THE HUMAN RESOURCES DEPARTMENT

Supervisors who work for large organizations that have professional Human Resources departments (personnel and training) have a big advantage when it comes to staffing new managers.

When it comes to hiring managers, professionals do most of the work of recruiting, testing, interviewing, orientation, training, and terminating. In some cases, all the supervisor needs to do is accept or reject a possible staff member sent for consideration.

It is important, however, that the supervisor do everything possible to maintain a good relationship with human resources experts. Fostering such a relationship includes the following activities:

- informing human resources and training specialists of the exact skills and competencies you need for maximum productivity,

- accepting the fact that human resources departments do their best to attract the most qualified applicants,

- abiding by equal opportunity laws and other legal restrictions, and

- paying compliments and offering feedback to those who get the right, properly trained people to you.

All employment decisions, including hiring, must follow Equal Employment Opportunity (EEO) guidelines. Employment laws are enforced by the federal EEOC. The supervisor must become acquainted with how EEOC impacts the organization and the supervisor. Employment decisions that ignore or violate EEO guidelines may result in costly litigation fees. Your Human Resources department can help explain these guidelines to you.

CONCLUSION

Most team members who quit will quit within the first 30 days of employment. Team members quit because they are not taught to be successful. Team member stability and high productivity often go together, but frequent personnel turnover is a fact of life in the hospitality industry. Team members quit because they feel unappreciated; they are not recognized and rewarded for their work. The goal of every supervisor should be to hire, develop, and maintain the most cohesive and productive staff possible. A supervisor should monitor the progress of a new team member until he or she has become a relaxed, full partner in the team and is making satisfactory progress toward maximum productivity. It is important that supervisors do everything possible to maintain a good relationship with human resources experts that work for the organization.

DISCUSSION QUESTIONS

1. As a supervisor, what are some ways you could decrease turnover in your operation?

2. What would you include in an orientation for new employees?

3. How would you prepare for interviewing job applicants? Would you use a direct interviewing approach or an indirect approach? Why?

4. Discuss the pros and cons of part-time employees in the hospitality industry.

5. As a supervisor, how would you interact with a Human Resources department?

PART IV

GETTING THE BEST
FROM YOUR TEAM

When your staff is performing well, you need to know how to keep them motivated and how to continue increasing productivity so your operation can be even more successful. In this part we look at strategies supervisors use, including fair compensation, delegation, and performance feedback.

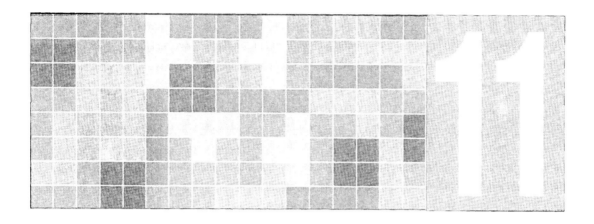

Paying
Your Team

Team members want to be fairly compensated for their productivity. When compensation is inequitable, staffing will never be right.

After you have finished reading this chapter, you should be able to

■ explain how team members should be compensated,

■ describe the four different stages of productivity, and

■ discuss the benefits of cross training team members.

YOU CAN AFFORD TO PAY THE GOOD TEAM MEMBERS

Too often in the hospitality industry, we link team member compensation to longevity. Longevity should be recognized and rewarded, but it is not necessarily a contributing factor to compensation. Some team members who have the longest tenure are often the same team members who are not the best performers, but they are being paid the highest wage. When this occurs, you are not spending your payroll wisely.

The industry often pays too much for new team members. New team members are often hired at rates higher than veteran team members are paid. When this happens, it causes dissent among team members, especially when the new team members are novices and veteran team members are training them.

Team members' pay should be based on performance. A novice should not be compensated as well as a seasoned employee. Pay should be linked to productivity and versatility.

Be prepared to defend salary to your team members when challenged. Discuss the matter privately. Justify salary by focusing on factors associated with performance. If your team members are not making the money they want to make, you should be able to tell them how their performance justifies their current pay and how they can improve their pay through better performance.

Do not discuss team members' specific pay rate with others. You should also instruct team members not to discuss their pay with other team members. (Unfortunately, most team members will not follow this directive. It is typical for team members to know what their fellow team members are being paid.)

Evaluating your staff's versatility using the four stages of productivity chart (see next page) allows you to determine the level of each team member's productivity, identify each team member's development needs, and determine the member's value to the department. This, in turn, helps you determine fair compensation for each of your employees. Furthermore, by minimizing turnover in Stages 3 and 4 you can retain your talented and experienced staff.

CROSS TRAINING

The two factors that determine a team member's wage are

1. how much money he or she is paid for each hour worked, and

2. the total number of hours he or she works.

The objective of every team member is to make as much money as possible. No matter how many raises you give, at some point you will max out the amount of money you can pay someone hourly. Once you hit your maximum hourly

STAGES OF PRODUCTIVITY

The contribution of team members defines productivity. This productivity can be categorized into four separate stages, as shown in the following table.

The Four Stages of Team Productivity

Stage 1	Stage 2	Stage 3	Stage 4
Novice—a team member who is limited in his or her ability to contribute to the operation	**Veteran**—a team member who performs the core functions of his or her job	**Specialist**—a team member who can aid the development of other team members and work with minimal supervision	**Entrepreneurial expert**—a team member who strives to improve his or her work productivity by contributing ideas on how to improve the work environment

Characteristics of Each Stage

Stage 1	Stage 2	Stage 3	Stage 4
Dependent on others	Assumes responsibility for his or her work assignment	Actively involved in developing other workers	Concerned about the operations as a whole, not just his or her immediate department
Developing job proficiencies	Creates ideas on how to make his or her job easier (path of least resistance)	Concerned about the contribution and impact of other team members on his or her work efforts	Eligible management candidate
Lacks confidence	Demonstrates expertise	Cross trained in more than one position	Exercises significant influence over critical organization decisions
Learning the basics of his or her position	Develops a procedural approach to his or her work	Demonstrates greater breadth of expertise	Formally influences the department's productivity
	Develops credibility and a reputation	Can handle additional assignments/projects	Often considered to be a lead team member
	Independently delivers results	Informally influences the department productivity	Provides feedback on the performance of other team members
		Often considered to be a core team member	Shares ideas for improving the operation/company
		Shares ideas for improving work area	

wage, the only way you can increase a person's wage in his or her current position is to increase the numbers of hours he or she works. This can be accomplished easily if the team member can excel in more than one position. Versatility gives the supervisor more options to schedule the team member for more hours because the person is able to work more positions. Also, many establishments will pay you more for learning more than one position. The more you are able to do, the more valuable you are.

Cross training provides many benefits to you as a supervisor. You can

- cover staff positions better during times of labor shortages,

- have more flexibility in scheduling team members,

- provide team members more hours based on their ability to work in more than one position,

- increase the wage of a team member based on his or her performance ability,

- minimize the need for you to become a micro leader, and

- reduce turnover.

TIPS FOR FAIR COMPENSATION

When you hire team members, they should work the schedule described to them during the hiring process. If your team members are consistently working more or less hours than they are scheduled, you are not appropriately planning for your staffing needs. This will affect your productivity, labor costs, and bottom line.

Here are some ways to ensure appropriate staffing levels and to ensure that your team is being fairly compensated:

- Train wait staff during the weekdays so that they can be polished and ready to earn more tips on the weekends. Start them out handling a small number of customers and gradually increase their area of responsibility.

- Kitchen, or back of the house, team members should start working at the beginning of the pay period. Doing this helps them to have a full check on their first paycheck.

- Eliminate overtime. There is no reason to have routine overtime. In fact, overtime is often a result of poor organization workflow or a disorganized supervisor. Examine the reasons for overtime. You might find that it is really for convenience rather than necessity, and you may be able to eliminate it by training team members, reassigning duties, and getting rid of operational bottlenecks.

- You are mismanaging your labor payroll if team members expect overtime as part of their regular compensation. Examine your schedule and the skill competencies of your team members and adjust accordingly.

- Use a staffing strategy. Observe the way your team members work and routinely analyze team members' workflow and productivity to make sure that your processes continue to make sense. Also be sure each staff member has the appropriate mix of skills to manage his or her responsibilities and can relieve other team members of work.

CONCLUSION

Team members' pay should be based on performance. Be prepared to defend salary to your team members when challenged. Discuss the matter privately. It is critical that supervisors do not discuss team members' specific pay rate with others. Cross training provides many benefits. If your team members are consistently working more or less hours than they are scheduled, you are not planning appropriately.

DISCUSSION QUESTIONS

1. Describe how you would assist a team member transition from productivity Stage 1 to Stage 4.

2. Explain why performance should be the driver of a person's compensation and not longevity.

3. How should a supervisor deal with team members who openly discuss their pay?

4. How can you eliminate paying overtime?

5. Discuss how you would implement a cross-training program for team members.

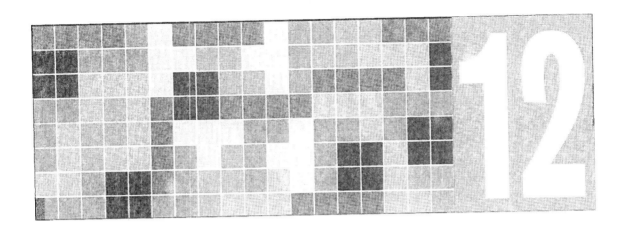

Delegation:
Sharing the Workload

After you have finished reading this chapter, you should be able to

◼ list five reasons why hospitality supervisors don't delegate responsibilities and duties often enough,

◼ describe the conditions under which a supervisor should delegate more, and

◼ describe in specific terms how to delegate.

Instead of working to develop the skills and abilities of their team members, most hospitality managers use their team members to subsidize their own work efforts.

The productivity of a team will always be greater than the productivity of their supervisor. Therefore, supervisors who spend their time educating, enabling, and empowering their team members to higher levels of productivity are more successful than managers who try to carry the bulk of the work themselves.

"Harry, turn some of that stuff over to your team members and relax a little."

"Sally, it's ridiculous for you to kill yourself doing such routine work when you have nine people in your department who need the experience."

"Come off it, Frank. You'd have plenty of time for more important things if you'd delegate some of those jobs you shouldn't be doing in the first place."

Question: Why do you work the grill every meal period?
Answer: My team is not capable of doing the work without my help.

Sound familiar? Yes, it's easy to tell others to delegate and it's true that most supervisors should delegate more, but most of us have to learn the lesson the hard way. Take Dee as an example.

Dee was a new, young, capable, and highly enthusiastic supervisor. She had five full-time and three part-time team members. Despite advice from all sides, she could not learn to assign work to others. Instead of delegating more, she simply pushed herself harder. Dee was so eager to be a successful supervisor that she was blind to what was happening. One of her best friends told her to manage more and do less. Her boss took her aside and gave her a heart-to-heart talk about the problem with little success.

One afternoon Dee passed out on the job and was taken by ambulance to a local hospital. The diagnosis was complete exhaustion. Dee hadn't received the message from her friends or boss, but she heard it loud and clear from her doctor. He put it very simply: She had to learn to reduce her workload.

Dee committed a critical mistake among hospitality supervisors. Instead of working harder to improve the productivity of her staff, Dee tried to improve her department productivity by working harder and longer hours herself. No matter how hard you work, you can only work a finite number of hours. Your body will eventually shut down if you constantly work like Dee. Supervisors like Dee burn out.

AVOIDING BURNOUT

Burnout is the result of physical and emotional exhaustion caused by prolonged stress due to working beyond what is healthy for you. Effective supervisors are aware of the symptoms of burnout and make every effort to adjust their load as the symptoms of burnout first begin to appear to them. The following chart lists some common symptoms of burnout.

The supervisor who begins to experience these symptoms is advised to seek ways to manage stress more effectively. Seeking medical attention may be necessary for those whose symptoms persists after proper adjustments in their workload have been made.

SYMPTOMS OF BURNOUT	
■ Feeling agitated	■ Loss of appetite
■ Begins to hate the job	■ Low enthusiasm/energy
■ Irritated by other staff members	■ Passes out on the job
■ Chest pains	■ Physical ailments
■ Difficulty sleeping	■ Physical exhaustion
■ Distrustful of other staff members	■ Poor decision making
■ Emotional exhaustion	■ Stomach pains
■ Excessive eating	■ Feeling stressed
■ Heart problems	■ Ulcers
■ Impatient with others	■ Walks out on the job
■ Lack of motivation	

DELEGATING AS PART OF A LARGER PLAN

To become more efficient and make better use of your time, you must conduct both a departmental and an individual job analysis. That is, you must step back and look at how your department is operating to reach your productivity goals. Then you must analyze all positions (including your own) to see how they can function better within the total operation.

As you do this analysis, consider the following:

■ Discontinue low-priority tasks. As with most situations, a few little things will not contribute to productivity or team member morale and can be eliminated. The same is true of time wasters that do not contribute to a happy working environment or your own positive attitude.

■ Delegate more of what is left. To free yourself for more important tasks, set up a running policy (utilizing the techniques presented in this chapter) of continuous delegation so that team members' abilities expand as you become more effective as a supervisor.

■ Be more efficient at what you do (see Chapters 15–20). As you prioritize your work and improve your own job skills, you will cut down on the time devoted to various aspects of your job. If such time and task management requires additional training on your part, enroll in whatever program will help. Ask your superior to recommend worthwhile training. We also recommend seeking a mentor, a person who can personally coach you.

■ Create and maintain a continuous learning environment. A culture where continuous training is expected will reduce errors, mistakes, and time wasters and raise productivity.

Leveraging Authority

Delegating primarily involves turning important work over to someone else. It means giving others the authority to complete an assignment while keeping the responsibility for the task being completed correctly. It means having sufficient faith in others to let them do important work for you.

Training directors for large organizations are in an excellent position to analyze and compare how supervisors delegate. Here are two penetrating comments.

> "When it comes to delegating, most inexperienced supervisors make two big mistakes: (1) they fail to do it skillfully and (2) they fail to delegate enough. Delegation of duties is difficult to put into practice."

> "The problem with delegating is that most supervisors know they should do it and most think they do, but few really do delegate and those who do often go about it awkwardly."

Delegating responsibilities and duties to others is necessary. Unless you learn to do it often and skillfully, your future as a manager may be seriously limited.

Why Leaders Fail to Delegate

Why do some hospitality supervisors fail to delegate as much as they should? The four basic reasons are all psychological in nature.

No Faith in Subordinates

Many supervisors do not see enough potential for success in the people who work for them and, as a result, never give their team members important and difficult assignments. Sometimes this kind of withholding happens because the supervisor has been burned in the past by poor performance; sometimes it is caused by unrealistic standards set by the supervisor. Most supervisors, however, simply lack confidence in the performance possibilities of team members. Unfortunately, this lack of confidence often results in poor performance when the supervisor is forced to delegate. To delegate successfully, you must have confidence in the results you anticipate and transmit this feeling to team members.

Fear of Superiors

Every time you delegate important work to others, you risk failure and possible criticism from your superiors. You lay your personal reputation on the line, which is as it should be. If you are not sufficiently secure in your job and company to risk a few failures, then you should not be a supervisor. Fear is a powerful emotion that can tie you up in knots and cause you to be too cautious. You must conquer fear before you can delegate freely and effectively.

Desire for Personal Credit

Some supervisors with a strong need for ego fulfillment try to do all the important work themselves so that they will receive personal credit from their superiors. In taking this narrow perspective, they fail to see that by relinquishing personal credit to their team members they can (through the motivation of other individuals) increase productivity, which, in turn, will improve the reputation of the department. It is shortsighted for a supervisor to want personal credit when departmental success ultimately will be more beneficial.

Misjudgment of Time

Many supervisors also are shortsighted about time. They refuse to take time to delegate responsibility today to free themselves for work that is more important next week. Time is the supervisor's most important commodity. If you refuse to delegate because doing it properly takes too much time, you are guilty of poor planning. Skillful delegating saves time.

Questions to Ask Yourself

Before turning your desire to delegate into an action plan, consider the following questions:

- Have you clearly identified the work that you should delegate?

- Have you chosen the right person? Does the team member want to do the new task?

- Knowing you remain responsible for results, how much decision-making authority are you willing to grant?

- What standards of performance will it take for you to be satisfied?

- What obstacles (if any) exist? How can they be overcome?

- Are you willing to spend the time required to train the person so that he or she produces at an acceptable level?

- Do you have a team member who has asked for more authority?

Know When to Keep It to Yourself or Delegate It

When should a leader delegate? You might wait forever for the perfect time to delegate; some delegation should take place under the following conditions:

1. When you need more time for work that only you can do, especially planning responsibilities that will contribute more to departmental productivity than the job being delegated

2. When delegating will help involve team members, improve their morale, and cause them to work closer to their potential

3. When it will not show undue favoritism or seriously damage relationships with other team members

4. When you are willing to take the time and effort to do a skillful job of delegating

5. When you are under pressure and must relinquish some responsibilities in order to protect your physical and mental health

How can you delegate skillfully? Everyone agrees that surfing, skydiving, and water skiing take skill, but few people acknowledge that the same is true of delegating. Delegating has its own special skill set; however, if you practice the following suggestions, you will greatly improve your ability to delegate.

Select the Task Carefully

Make a priority list of assignments you might delegate. For a job to qualify for this list, it should be taking too much of your time, low in responsibility compared to your other duties, and motivating for your team members. Do not just delegate those tasks that you are bored with and that you are sure your team member will find boring as well. Once you have your list, start from the top and delegate one task at a time. Try to spread tasks among your team members until you sense you are reaching a saturation point.

Select the Person Carefully

Consider all factors involved before selecting the person to whom you will give a specific task. Which team members have too much or too little work to do? Does any particular individual need a special challenge? Will the individual you select accept it with enthusiasm? Does the person have the training and talent to execute it well? How will co-workers react? Will it increase departmental productivity? Obviously, you must know your team members well if assignments are to fit the special needs and talents of each.

Prepare All Individuals for Change

Because sudden, unannounced changes can disturb people and hurt productivity, announce your decisions in order to protect your relationships with all team members and give the team member receiving the assignment all possible assistance. In most cases, a group announcement is best so that everyone is informed, misunderstandings are minimized, and an opportunity to ask questions is provided. In delegating, you must be concerned with the feelings of all team members, not just those of the person to whom you are delegating.

Turn Over the Assignment

Consider the following steps in turning over new responsibilities to a team member:

1. Meet in private where you will not be interrupted.

2. Allocate sufficient time to go over the new job step by step. Illustrate or demonstrate tasks whenever possible.

3. Ask the team member for verbal feedback on all details presented to eliminate future misunderstandings.

4. Give the team member an opportunity to ask questions.

5. Compliment the team member on previous work and transmit your confidence in the way she or he will perform the new responsibility.

6. Set a time and date for follow-up; however, it is often best to find out how the team member is doing before the due date.

7. Monitor task progress, but let the team member do the task without your interference or control.

8. Make yourself available to answer questions, provide guidance, or give additional training and reassurance.

Provide Follow-Up

Soon after delegating, make yourself available to answer further questions and provide additional training. Questions similar to these often facilitate communications:

■ How are you doing on the new equipment?

■ How do you feel now about your new assignment?

■ Do you need any help I have not provided?

■ Do you have any suggestions for me or other team members?

To delegate without follow-up is to ask for trouble and disappointment. You can delegate authority, but not your responsibility. All team members share the final responsibility for results, but the supervisor must take the greatest percentage. If you learn to delegate frequently and skillfully, you will eventually worry less, feel less pressured, have more time to plan and organize, build better relationships with your team members, and motivate greater productivity in your department.

THE BIG PICTURE—LEARNING AND LIVING

Delegating correctly to your team members allows you to pursue other endeavors. The time you gain can be used to improve the quality of your life. What will you do with the time you save? Here are some suggestions:

1. Spend more time improving professional relationships.

2. Start solving problems before they occur.

3. Do departmental planning.

4. Learn new skills by investing in your own development.

5. Seek opportunities to receive more responsibility from your supervisor.

6. Plan and pursue your next career opportunity.

Delegation is a powerful tool for empowerment. Research shows that challenging work is highly motivating. Giving more responsibility to your followers creates greater challenges, and this ultimately makes a more powerful, productive work team.

CONCLUSION

The productivity of a team will always be greater than the productivity of their supervisor. Burnout is the result of physical and emotional exhaustion caused by prolonged stress due to working beyond what is healthy for you. To become more efficient and make better use of your time, you must conduct both a departmental and an individual job analysis. Delegating primarily involves turning important work over to someone else. In delegating, you must be concerned with the feelings of all team members, not just those of the person to whom you are delegating. To delegate without follow-up is to ask for trouble and disappointment.

DISCUSSION QUESTIONS

1. Develop a profile of an individual who, because of job skills, might be willing to take on extra work duties.

2. Would most team members be happier and produce more if they were given more authority by their managers? Why or why not?

3. Why do so many supervisors use lack of time as an excuse for not delegating? How would you convince such a person that spending time now could save time later?

4. Describe a task that your supervisor could delegate to you that would reduce his or her workload and provide you with the opportunity to learn.

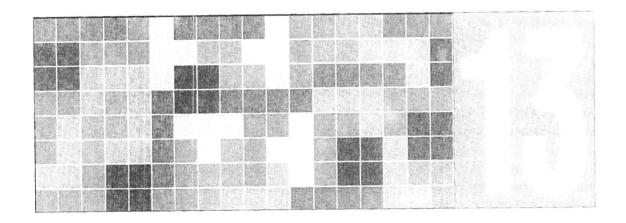

Teaching Others What You Know

Spend your time working to educating, enabling, and empowering your team members. Spend your time teaching them to do what you do.

After you have finished reading this chapter, you should be able to

■ apply the four-step teaching formula,

■ describe the four types of power supervisors have, and

■ list the reasons why training is a motivational tool.

As a hospitality supervisor, you are endowed with a certain undeniable power. This power originates from four sources:

1. *Role power* gives you the influence you need to assert your authority. It must be used wisely. In the beginning, team members tend to associate a certain level of respect with your position. Understand it is the position they are respecting, not necessarily you. You earn respect over time.

THE BEST WAYS TO EARN RESPECT

■ Give respect to your team members.

■ Demonstrate your willingness to assist them when they need help.

■ Share credit and spread recognition.

■ Give of yourself by supporting team members' interests and addressing their concerns.

---

2. *Personality power* is the second source of power. You should use your personality to encourage greater productivity and accomplish other tasks. Remember, a positive leader will usually out coach a negative leader. Your operations will adopt your personality. The attitude and personality you bring to work is contagious; your mood establishes the climate you experience. Leaders who are positive, friendly, and have a customer service–oriented demeanor will cultivate the same style of behavior in team members.

3. *People power* is the third source of your power. The success of your establishment is directly linked to your ability to develop and maintain a team environment. Keep in mind that a group of individuals working together is not necessarily displaying teamwork.

    ■ Focus on improving performance through training and recognition.

    ■ Address people who fail to perform. Expect various team members to complain and announce their dissent when you are challenging them to raise their performance bar.

    ■ Set the pace for success. It is unlikely that the members of your team will work with the same drive as you, and many managers become disappointed when their team members don't exhibit the same drive they have. Your goal should be to move team members from where they are to where you want them to be.

- Recruit team members who elevate the performance of the team. Some teams are involved in interviewing prospective applicants.
- You must monitor the climate, morale, and influences affecting your team's performance. Intervene when necessary to improve performance.

4. *Knowledge power* is the most important and underestimated source of power you possess. You may not have viewed it this way in the past, but teaching your staff new ideas, skills, and competencies gives you prestige (and power) in their eyes.

   Team members usually take pride in learning something new and doing it well. When you make learning possible, you earn their respect and build enduring, productive relationships. As a supervisor, you have daily opportunities to use your knowledge power.

TIMES TO USE YOUR KNOWLEDGE POWER

- Every time you have to assume the duties of a team member in order to maintain the success of the department, someone should benefit from your efforts. Train someone every time you have to work to maintain operations.
- The best hospitality supervisors are always walking and talking. As you tour your facility, observe the activities of your team members. Praise what is right. Train to eliminate errors.
- Train anytime there is a new procedure to be learned.
- Train team members until they are capable of training other team members.

HOW TO TEACH BY NOT TEACHING

Frequently the supervisor is the only person who teaches the many skills new team members need to learn: how to operate machines, how to complete forms, the need to understand procedures, how to work skillfully with difficult customers, how to maintain equipment, and so on. On-the-job learning never stops.

You can become an outstanding on-the-job instructor without employing any of the formal methods we usually associate with the traditional classroom teacher. All supervisors are models, and to a surprising extent your team members will adjust their behavior and model yours. Team members are always watching you, so everything you do teaches something.

While team members learn a great deal from you without your knowing it, they also need specific help from you, and you want to provide this help in your own style without being labeled a "teacher." Instead of saying to a new team member, "Let me teach you how to do this," it might be better to say, "Let me show you how I can make your job easier." Instead of saying to a regular team member, "Let me teach you to do it right the first time," it might be better to say, "Let me show you how I do this and then you can figure out the best way for you to do it."

YOUR ATTITUDE TOWARD TEACHING

What is your personal attitude toward sharing your knowledge with team members? Are you willing to set aside enough time to do it professionally? Do you desire to build a good reputation as a patient, caring instructor? Are you more like Marvin or Mary?

> Marvin accepts a new team member into his department regardless of how much experience the individual has. When assuming his teaching role, he is patient, positive, and thorough, even if the team member is slow to catch on. As a result, Marvin develops a cohesive, productive, and loyal staff. His patient teaching attitude is admired and respected, especially by those from other cultures.

> Mary consistently complains that new team members should have learned more in school. She shows little patience in teaching others. As a result, her staff makes more mistakes and personnel turnover is high. New team members are often forced to go to co-workers for help they need. Mary's negative attitude toward teaching others creates problems instead of solving them.

A FOUR-STEP TRAINING PROCESS FOR ON-THE-JOB TRAINING

For years, professional instructors have followed a four-step teaching process that is best used for conducting practical on-the-job training (OJT) . You may wish to view this process as a baseball game; you have four bases to cover before you can score in OJT.

First Base: Prepare the Team Member

Put the team member at ease. Give the person time to adjust to you personally before you move into teaching the job. Find out a little more about the team member, make small talk, and try to put the person at ease. Make the effort to establish a relaxed learning climate. It is time well spent. Once the team member is comfortable, use the following ideas:

1. State the job you are going to teach and find out what the team member already knows about it. Do not waste time (or insult the team member) by teaching something he or she already knows. You may discover that a quick review is all that is necessary.

2. Make training your priority. Most people are motivated to learn new tasks. Continuous learning is often associated with high productivity and job satisfaction. Explain the benefits of learning new tasks to your team member. You might suggest that it could help the individual earn the respect of others and earn more money by increasing his or her value to the organization.

Talk about the personal satisfaction and pride that can come from learning something new. Learning something new can be exciting. Your job as a teacher will be much easier if the team member wants to learn.

3. Place the team member in the correct learning position. Just as a baseball player must have the right stance to hit the ball, it might be best for the team member to be at your left side instead of your right. Determine the best physical position for the team member in each job you teach and be certain that he or she is located properly before you start. Attention to this factor will make the job easier for you and the team member.

4. Ask the trainee how he or she learns best and how he or she would like to learn the tasks. Design the training to fit the learning style of the trainee whenever possible. For example, some trainees may want to have a manual to refer to when they have questions or problems; others may want the supervisor or trainer readily available to answer their questions when need arises.

Second Base: Present the Operation

Now you are ready to try for second. The following suggestions will take you there with little difficulty:

1. Describe, illustrate, and demonstrate one important step in a task at a time. Do not give so much information at once that the team member becomes confused. This may not be easy because you know the job so well that it's hard for you to remember how long it took you to learn it. Stress safety! Demonstrate the use of safety procedures, the use of equipment, and the wearing of safety clothing or gear.

2. Tell the team member how to do the job, speaking clearly and slowly. Use simple words. If you must use a technical term, be sure to explain what you mean, and whenever possible, follow up with an illustration. Take out your pencil and sketch the process; it need not be a work of art to convey the message. Show the team member by actually performing the job yourself one step at a time. Be sure that you perform the task in complete detail so that your actions are easily observed. Never show trainees how NOT to do the task. If you do, they may only remember what you showed them and forget that it was incorrect. Showing only the correct way do something is especially important when demonstrating safety maneuvers. Always show the correct way so no one gets hurt.

3. Stress the one key point in each step of the operation as you go through the process. This emphasis will help the team member recall each step later by remembering the key points, and the process will become easier. When a given job takes more than five steps, this procedure becomes increasingly important.

4. Instruct clearly, completely, and patiently, but do not give the team member more than can be mastered. The greatest error that most supervisors commit is trying to teach too much too fast. They overestimate their teaching abilities and the team member's learning ability. If you try to teach too much at one

time, you will only confuse the team member, and you will have to start over. Break the total job into separate steps and present them in sequence. Do not start the second step until the first step has been mastered. If necessary, permit a lapse of time between steps. Focus on teaching the material thoroughly, even though time is at a premium.

Third Base: Supervise a Trial Performance

Give the new team member an immediate opportunity to do the job on a trial basis following this three-step procedure:

1. Have the trainee do the job so that you can correct errors quickly. Few new trainees perform jobs perfectly the first time, and the only way to spot errors is to have the team member try out the process under your direction. Of course, errors should be pointed out and corrected quickly without showing impatience.

2. Have the trainee explain the key points of the job. It is important to have him or her repeat the key points learned at second base verbally during the first performance; explaining each one makes it easier to remember.

3. Make sure the trainee understands. It is vital that he or she understand why it is best to do a job in a certain way and why the job is important to the total efficiency of the department. Give the trainee the opportunity to ask questions. If necessary, continue the dry runs until the skill is mastered.

Home Base: The Follow-Up

1. Allow the trainee to do the task, but provide support and tell the person where to go for help. If you are not easily accessible, find someone who can help new co-workers learn and keep a high level of productivity. Appoint someone who will be compatible with the new team member and is willing to help when needed.

2. Check frequently to see if all is going well. Take time to check with the team member. Nothing can replace your own interest during the team member's first critical days of learning.

3. Taper off gradually so that the team member does not feel oversupervised. After a certain point, the trainee deserves the satisfaction and freedom of going it alone. Stepping back will provide the team member with the confidence needed to assume further responsibility at a later date. Oversupervising can destroy initiative. Pull away when your job performance standards have been met.

If you successfully follow these steps, your chances of success will be greatly enhanced. The team member will know how to do the job; he or she will do it right the first time and have the confidence to be a long-term, productive member of your department. You will have begun to establish a solid relationship.

If you have tried the four basic steps and still feel that you have failed in your efforts to train, the cause could be one or more of the following three errors:

1. Failure to devote enough time to training. You must allow sufficient time to do the teaching job properly, even if it means putting aside some of your other responsibilities temporarily. It will not be easy to do, but the long-range productivity of your team members will prove that you have spent your time well.

2. Failure to follow the system step by step. The system provided in this chapter takes time, but it works. If you skip a step, the system will break down.

3. Failure to show enough patience with the slow team member. Few new team members will be as experienced as you would like them to be. Some may learn more slowly than others. When you must teach a slow team member to do a job, you must slow your own pace or the results will be disappointing. Cover each of the four bases with special patience and consideration, even if it means taking twice as much time as you devoted in the past. Keep in mind that slow team members can become excellent producers once they master the job, so the extra time you devote now will not be wasted.

DELEGATING TRAINING RESPONSIBILITIES

Professional educators frequently admit that the best way to learn to do something well is to teach it. At times, you may wish to delegate the training of a new team member to a regular team member who fully understands and practices the four-step process effectively. By delegating, you will give recognition to the regular team member, provide excellent training to the new team member, and save yourself time. It may be wise, however, for you to retain the follow-up responsibility to make certain that the team member you selected as a trainer does the job correctly. Be sure to train the trainer in the use of the four-step training process.

GROUP INSTRUCTION

As well as training your own new individual team members, you may be invited to make a presentation to other supervisors and your superiors. You can prepare for the event by making one or more group presentations to your team members. Follow the same basic steps you use in individual instruction: Prepare the group (first base), present the new material (second base), gain involvement through questions (third base), and summarize (home base) by repeating the goal of the meeting.

As you follow these basic principles, you also might consider the following:

1. The more simple visual aids you prepare in advance, the more confidence you will have in your presentation and the more effective you will be.

2. Lecturing is the least effective teaching method, so strive for as much group interaction as possible.

3. Cover your subject carefully by outlining your instructions from start to finish.

4. Get your hands dirty. It's one thing to talk about the work; it's another thing to do the work. People learn best by doing the job they are expected to perform.

CONCLUSION

Training never stops. As long as you must cope with an ever-increasing number of changes, you must accumulate new knowledge and pass on what you have learned to those who work for you. Everyone, including your superiors, finds it stressful to keep up with changes both in the environment in general and within the organization in particular. You will need to train yourself to deal with the impact of change, which means you will need to learn new ways to perform responsibilities. The greater the changes, the more you must learn; the more you learn, the more time you must spend instructing others and preparing them for change.

Changes manifest themselves in different ways: New procedures, new techniques, new generations of computers, new employees, and new ways of dealing with problems. As changes occur, you should occasionally search for fresh ideas and procedures to put into your own personal "knowledge bag." You should continue to educate yourself through both self instruction and formal course programs. When you learn something that will improve the productivity of your department, pass it on to your staff using the four-step method.

DISCUSSION QUESTIONS

1. Assume that you are going to start training a new team member on baking bread. How would you implement the four-step system?

2. From your experience as a team member, do you feel that supervisors, generally speaking, are good instructors? Cite examples to support your view.

3. How can supervisors or team leaders train themselves to spend sufficient time on quality instruction that will earn respect from all team members? Be specific.

4. How would a new manager take advantage of his or her sources of power? When can the use of power become abusive?

5. Identify a problem occurring on your shift. Determine if it is related to or due to lack of training. Design and deliver the training and reassess the problem. Is it still there?

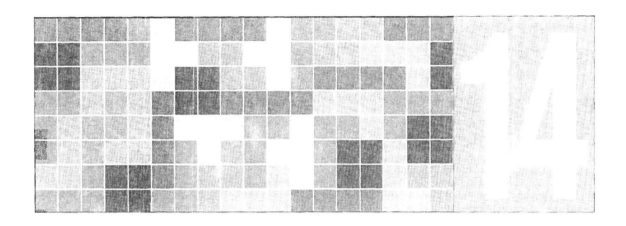

Evaluating Performance: The Formal Appraisal

When interviewed about their position, 80% of American managers cannot answer with any measure of confidence these seemingly simple questions:

- What is my job?
- What in it really counts?
- How well am I doing?

—W. Edwards Deming

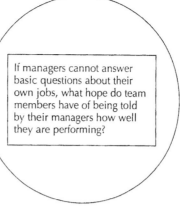

If managers cannot answer basic questions about their own jobs, what hope do team members have of being told by their managers how well they are performing?

After you have finished reading this chapter, you should be able to

■ apply the techniques to link appraisals to performance objectives,

■ identify the benefits of a formal performance review and the importance of being truthful when discussing your team members' performance, and

■ describe how to use performance reviews in a positive way, and

■ describe how to provide constructive feedback.

Assessment of team members' performance must occur every day. One of the most important responsibilities of a hospitality supervisor is to recognize and respond to performance, be it good or bad. Team members should know how they are doing on a daily basis and be exposed to constant feedback on their performance. It should not come as a surprise to anyone how his or her performance compares to known, expected objectives when it is time to assess performance formally. In the appraisal we are only recapping what should have been previously shared.

In most sizable organizations, hospitality supervisors formally assess the performance of each of their team members every 6 or 12 months. If you have been on the receiving end of such an appraisal, you probably still remember the manager, the printed instrument, the interview, and the results. The purpose of this chapter is to prepare you to administer such evaluations for the first time or to help you improve upon the way you have handled them in the past.

Different organizations follow different procedures. Some require team members to evaluate themselves first and then let the supervisor react. Some require the supervisor to rate the team members first and then let them react. Some leave it totally up to the manager.

Regardless of the system (and each has advantages), you should openly discuss the rating with the team member, explaining and, if necessary, defending your position on all factors rated. Try to establish a two-way conference in which the team member has a free and fair chance to present his or her case. An appraisal without this two-way conference may be in compliance with the procedure, but it is a mockery of its purpose. Important employment decisions are based on documented performance. Pay raises, promotions, transfers, and layoffs are serious matters and often are determined by one's performance appraisal.

Supervisors need to know how to appraise performance and how to conduct the appraisal conference so that the appraisal is accurate. If your company has a training program on this topic, take advantage of the opportunity and attend. Often local colleges put on seminars related to management or supervision, and performance appraisal is generally included as a topic.

In the meantime, here are a few suggestions:

- Observe performance daily.

- Consistently follow-up with team members each time you give a directive or observe their work.

- Document your observations and subsequent activities.

- Based on your documentation, give specific examples to justify a performance rating.

- Share details on how to improve/maintain team members' performance.

- Provide your team members with specific examples of the behaviors you are evaluating. For example, if you are evaluating a team member's attitude or initiative, be sure to communicate the behaviors that you think fall into these categories.

- Do not be late in giving the appraisal; it is too important to be postponed or delayed. If the appraisal is late, the team member may conclude that performance is not important to the supervisor.

LINKING APPRAISALS TO PERFORMANCE OBJECTIVES

Formal appraisals must evaluate performance against known performance objectives. For example, your superior might tie your appraisal to the success you have had in reaching the goals and objectives you submitted at an earlier time. If you have made excellent progress toward the approved goals, chances are good that you will receive a positive report. Factors that may be considered in a supervisor's review include human relations skills, dependability, and the ability to handle problem team members.

In a sense, a formal appraisal is a form of accountability. You are asked to account for your past performance based on certain standards that are included on the rating sheet. As we said, in a majority of organizations, salary increases, bonuses, and other forms of compensation are tied to the performance rating. Results, therefore, are critical to those being appraised.

BENEFITS TO MANAGEMENT

Management has good reasons for supporting the appraisal program and insisting that all people (including themselves) be measured occasionally under a standardized procedure. Here are some of those reasons:

1. It is the best way to make sure that the high-production team member is identified and recognized and that the low-production team member is located and counseled.

2. Properly administered by the supervisor, the system builds a stronger working relationship between the supervisor and the team member, and that helps improve performance.

3. The policy produces a more objective basis for salary increases and promotions.

4. A formal system, though never perfect, will provide better and more uniform treatment of individuals by management than having no system.

5. The review process provides organizations with the help they need to maintain and improve standards.

6. Formal appraisal provides the supervisor the opportunity to communicate what is expected of team members in the performance of their job.

7. A formal appraisal creates a record of a team member's performance that can be retained as documentation in a person's personnel file.

Management should be the first to recognize that the key to the success of the appraisal system is its administration. For this reason, supervisors are being given more and more training to make the system work.

BENEFITS TO TEAM MEMBERS

It is easy to see why management endorses a good appraisal system that is properly administered, but what about its benefits to team members? Do they really come out ahead? In the great majority of cases, the answer is yes for the following reasons:

1. The procedure clarifies what is expected of the team member.

2. It provides a system of recognition and prevents team members from being ignored or lost.

3. It forces the supervisor to discuss work performance in relationship to expectations, thus creating a more objective and open relationship with the team member.

4. The system helps the team member pinpoint weak areas so that improvements can be made.

5. It forces periodic communication between the supervisor and the team member.

RATING FAIRLY

With all your other responsibilities, you may be tempted to back away from an honest appraisal of your people by giving them a better rating than they deserve. This is sometimes referred to as the error of leniency. This may also occur when the supervisor wants to be liked. Team members know how they perform better than you do and will lose respect for you if you are too lenient—especially if you fail to assess accurately the performance of team members who routinely perform at less than desired results. Most team members want an accurate evaluation and may feel shortchanged and disappointed if you do not give it to them. You also owe it to the other members of your team to be truthful. Team members already know how their performance matches up to their peers. As a supervisor you must distinguish good and bad performers accurately.

- *Know and be prepared to discuss performance standards.* When assessing a team member's performance, you must be able to explain how that person's performance compares to the performance standard. If someone performs above or below a performance standard, you must be able to specify how. Sharing the details helps team members know what they did right or wrong and why they are exceptional or at risk.

- *Be sure to be objective.* A minimal rating or a high mark given grudgingly may leave the team member feeling unappreciated. Motivation to produce can drop dramatically if team members sense that you are not objective.

- *Don't appraise personalities.* Remember that you are appraising the team member's performance, not his or her personality. Base your evaluation on objective data such as following procedures, productivity, competence, attendance records, customer service, cooperativeness, and flexibility.

- *Avoid basing your evaluation on the potential of the team member rather than on actual performance.* Evaluate what the team member contributed to the unit's productivity, not what he or she is capable of contributing.

- *Base your evaluation on the team member's average performance during the period covered, not on isolated examples of extremely good or bad work.* One good or bad day, week, or month shouldn't necessarily result in a corresponding high or low rating.

- *Avoid the halo effect.* No one is perfect. Be careful of a tendency to rate someone as being excellent in all categories.

- *Avoid the error of central tendency, in which you select the middle rating on all factors.* Supervisors can fall into this trap when they are in a hurry or want to play it safe because they do not want to accept the responsibility of justifying a high rating or a low rating.

THE APPRAISAL

The modern approach to performance appraisals differs from the traditional approach in both emphasis and content. Some of the distinguishing characteristics of the modern approach follow:

- The salary-wage interview is often separate from the performance improvement interview so that salary does not dominate the discussion.

■ The performance appraisal is future oriented instead of focusing on past re-sults. It may identify training or development needs.

■ Emphasis is placed on the establishment of work objectives that can be achieved by the next evaluation period, not on criticism about past performance.

■ The basic idea is to develop a supportive climate and improve the relation-ship between the supervisor and the team member through nonevaluative listening, nondirective counseling, and performance feedback.

Performance appraisal consists of two parts the, content and the conference. Let us consider content first.

Part 1: Content—The Form

You cannot accomplish an appraisal without using a form or rating sheet that be-comes a documented record. There are almost as many different appraisal instru-ments as there are organizations that use them. Few, if any, fully satisfy the people who designed them or the supervisors who use them. Almost any form, however, can be used effectively if the supervisor uses the tips described in this chapter.

The content is the information on the appraisal form itself. A typical form includes its purpose, instructions on how to fill it out, and where copies are to go. It contains the behavior categories being assessed and the ratings scales by which performance is measured.

The supervisor should give the team member a copy of the form at the be-ginning of the rating period so they both may refer to it from time to time. This form will contain information on performance characteristics on which a team member may be rated. These characteristics should contain complete definitions and clarification of exactly what behaviors the supervisor puts in the category. For example, the performance characteristic "dependability" could have many behaviors associated with it. Those behaviors the supervisor thinks fall in this category need to be communicated to the team member at the beginning and during the rating period, not just at the end when team members receive their performance appraisals. If the manager does not convey clear behavioral expec-tations of "dependability," team members have to guess as to what the manager thinks dependability is, and they may guess wrong.

The rating scale also should be considered carefully because it has serious pit-falls. Values commonly used to measure a team member's performance include

■ Exceptional ■ Very Good ■ Good ■ Fair ■ Unacceptable

Most managers find it easy to explain the differences between "Exceptional" per-formance and "Unacceptable" performance because they are the extremes. How-ever, many experience difficulty explaining the difference between "Fair" performance and "Good" performance. Trouble brews when a team member asks what exactly he or she must do to move from the lower rating of "Fair" to the higher rating of "Good." If the supervisor cannot tell team members what they must do to improve, team members may wonder exactly how the supervisor ar-rived at that rating in the first place.

Part 2: The Conference

The second part of the performance appraisal is the conference.

Many team members complain that their appraisal form is completed by their supervisor and merely handed to them for their signature without a personal or private conference. The team member is left out of the process entirely. Leaving the team member out is a big mistake. As mentioned earlier, performance appraisals have enormous effects on team members, and they expect and deserve a professionally conducted review.

Conferences take time and skill. A professional appraisal will have the following characteristics:

- A supervisor should conduct the appraisal. One's immediate supervisor is usually the person who directly observes the performance of a team member. Team members are skeptical of a review done by someone who does not see their work.

- During the review, the supervisor should allow time for questions and an opportunity for the team member to provide input into his or her final rating. This process takes open, two-way communication. The manager needs to listen and be open to changing his or her rating during the discussion. Hurrying through the conference will not accomplish its purpose. To rush the procedure is to destroy it; you must make time to do it properly.

- The appraisal is a confidential matter between the supervisor and team member. It should be done in a quiet, private place. The review meeting deserves time, giving the team member the opportunity to thoroughly discuss his or her performance. The talk: listen ratio should be balanced or in favor of the team member; the supervisor should do most of the listening and the team member most of the talking.

Using the Appraisal Process as a Positive Tool

Appraisals give you an opportunity to use your communication skills. You should apply the five R's of private communications covered in Chapter 8. Reviews should be viewed as a positive experience—something you can learn to do well now that will serve you well as you move into higher management roles.

Managers usually take one of two positions when it comes to formal reviews.

1. Those who understand the importance of performance reviews and have been trained to give them see the value in the process and turn it into a positive tool. Their team members look forward to it.

2. Those who fear the process or who are not adequately trained fight the process most of the way. Their team members resent the procedure as much as their supervisors do.

You as the rater determine the success or failure of any appraisal system; you can look forward to every review situation or you can try to avoid it. How you handle the appraisal will determine whether your team members consider it an opportunity or a chore.

The positive approach pays off for supervisors because they use the appraisal system to improve productivity in their departments. They take advantage of the procedure to build better relationships with their people, and they make it a vehicle to get raises and promotions for their better team members.

The first time a team member is formally appraised can be extremely important to both the individual and the organization. Take extra time to explain the purpose and procedure, go over the form in detail so that no misunderstandings remain, and make sure that the team member has an opportunity to ask questions and to feel comfortable with the procedure.

Follow these guidelines to make your appraisal system a positive experience:

- Introspective self-evaluation is a primary purpose of any appraisal program. It is not a tool to embarrass, intimidate, dispose of, annoy, or harass a team member. It is designed to help the team member gauge his or her progress and future with the company. Geared to the needs of the team member, the system cannot fail; geared exclusively to the needs of the organization, it becomes suspect and loses its value.

- Many appraisal systems seem overcomplicated with too much detail. Even so, try to work within the system by following the instructions carefully. Follow the necessary red tape without griping. The system depends on the supervisor to make it effective.

- Sometimes you may be so enthusiastic over an outstanding appraisal that you either make or imply a promise that you cannot keep in a reasonable length of time. Nothing lowers morale faster than a broken promise. Therefore, you must protect everyone by making only accurate statements that cannot be misinterpreted.

- To evaluate fairly the performance of another person is a sensitive, difficult process. Realize that it is never easy to separate performance from personality, and accept all available help to keep the procedure from backfiring and causing serious human relation problems. The suggestions presented here will help you stay on the right track, but they cannot remove the responsibility of the ultimate rating decision from your shoulders. You are the only one close enough to the team member to have all the necessary facts and data, who can provide the quality counseling that must accompany the process.

- When you must give an unsatisfactory rating, make sure you follow these steps:
  1. Have all the facts at your disposal.
  2. Discuss the problem with the team member.
  3. Share your decision with both your superior and the human resource department.
  4. Be ready to recognize an improvement in productivity if and when it happens.

■ Do not be late giving the appraisal. Late appraisals may cause a delay in a raise, promotion, or other important employment decision for the team member. Do it on time or before the last possible due date. If appraisals are routinely late in coming, team members may conclude that performance does not matter to the manager, and this may result in lower productivity or job dissatisfaction.

■ Do not convey to the team member that once the regular appraisal is over no further help or counseling will occur until the next time. If the appraisal was positive, the team member may feel you will ignore future problems. If it was negative, he or she may feel that you will not be available for more help until the next appraisal session. Good follow-up procedures are essential to the success of the system.

GIVING CONSTRUCTIVE FEEDBACK

The supervisor is responsible for establishing and maintaining an environment where employees can produce their best work. There are many characteristics of a motivating environment just as there are many characteristics of a healthy flower garden. One important characteristic is providing constructive feedback. Giving your team members constructive feedback is certainly important during the formal performance appraisal. Constructive feedback on performance is the cornerstone of personal growth and development. An effective leader is one who can communicate to his or her followers using constructive feedback techniques. Being able to give and receive constructive feedback is a tool that belongs in every supervisor's survival kit. Conducted skillfully, constructive feedback can strengthen the quality of any relationship. It can also change behavior when nothing else works.

A constructive feedback session is more than a casual discussion resulting from an accidental encounter. It is a serious, two-way communication initiated by either the team member or the supervisor. The reason may be a formal one, such as completing the team member's annual performance appraisal, or trying to change inappropriate behavior using the disciplinary procedure.

A constructive feedback session may be used when dealing with a situation that may become a problem if not talked about. The purposes of the session are to increase productivity by avoiding or solving problems and to strengthen or repair working relationships. Feedback sessions

■ involve sitting down in some private place and getting job problems out in the open by talking, listening, and trying to understand the other person's point of view

■ involve working out solutions that everyone involved can accept

Constructive feedback is *not* constructive criticism. In fact, criticism is rarely constructive at all. To illustrate, movie critics may give a movie two thumbs down. This means that in their estimation, the movie was bad. It does not convey to the director of the movie why the rating was given, nor does it give advice on how to improve the movie. It is simply the critic's evaluation of the movie. The director is left to guess why the movie was given two thumbs down. He may become defensive or upset at the criticism, discount its importance, or criticize the critics for being incompetent.

Constructive feedback, on the other hand, is descriptive, not just evaluative. For example, in constructive feedback on the quality of his movie, the director may be told that during the opening scene of his western set in the 1880s there appears to be a faint shadow of an airplane flying over. With this type of specific information the director can learn from the constructive feedback and make better pictures in the future.

Constructive feedback is achieved by dividing feedback into four categories:

1. **State the observable behavior(s) or action:** Tell your team member the behavior you observed.

    Example: "This morning you told a guest that she could not have extra towels to use at the pool."

2. **Determine the reason behind the behavior:** Ask for reasons why the team member behaved in this way. Allow the team member to tell you why he or she said this to a guest.

3. **Explain the effects of observed behavior:** Let the team member know how his or her behavior affects the organization. If the behavior does not affect the organization in any important way, it may be best to forget about it.

4. **Provide an appropriate alternative behavior:** Let your team know how they should have responded to the guest so they can do so in the future.

Constructive feedback should be given in private. Properly given, constructive feedback is much appreciated by team members. Responsible employees want to do the right thing and will make efforts to correct behavior when given the opportunity. If the inappropriate behavior continues after receiving constructive feedback, the supervisor may need to take disciplinary action.

Remember that constructive feedback is a very appropriate and effective tool for reinforcing correct or exemplary performance.

PERSONAL PERFORMANCE CONTRACTS

One of the main purposes of the performance appraisal is to provide feedback on performance. When improvement is warranted, the supervisor and his team member may find that a personal performance contract (PPC) is the right tool for the job.

A PPC is a written document of agreement that establishes future goals for which a team member becomes accountable. It forecasts accomplishments to be achieved within a specific time period. It will contain specific types of support that the supervisor will provide in order to help the team member reach his or her goals. If at all possible, positive tangible benefits, such as increased salary, should be tied to the accomplishment of the goals stated in the personal performance contract. Here are the normal steps taken in the development of a PPC:

1. Write out the specific needs or goals to be accomplished.

2. List the top three objectives that become the essence of the contract.

3. Gain the approval of your supervisor.

4. Develop an action plan so that both parties will know what the team member will be doing over a given time frame.

5. Emphasize the self-development aspects of any contract.

6. Conduct reviews to ensure steady progress.

7. Remember that any contract is a two-way street. Whether the team member reaches his or her goals may depend on your contribution to the contract.

APPRAISALS AND CAREER PLANNING

It is inevitable that going through the evaluation process frequently causes team members to review their own career progress or master plans. More than anything else, an appraisal tells a person how he or she is doing and whether that person should make adjustments to work behavior and performance. It is a time of self-evaluation.

As a supervisor, you will want to tie your appraisals to planning the future of your team members. If they receive weak appraisals, what can they do to make improvements before the next period arrives? What self-improvement projects might they undertake to eliminate deficiencies?

> Mrs. Henry runs the group tour department for the Bountiful Foods Corporation with a staff of 50. This year she decided to give individual raises based on performance appraisals instead of giving across the board increases. She viewed this responsibility as a challenge that could increase staff productivity by communicating to each individual exactly how they contributed to the operation and, most important, their specific areas of strengths and weaknesses. Mrs. Henry spent considerable time preparing each appraisal.
>
> Her first appraisal was with Amir, a group tour guide, who was highly dependable and capable of working with minimal supervision. Mrs. Henry rated Amir excellent in every category but cooperativeness. In recent months, Amir had become irritated with others in a variety of situations.
>
> Under Mrs. Henry's gentle probing, Amir admitted that he was frequently upset over the poor attitudes and performance of other workers he thought were paid substantially more than he. When Mrs. Henry suggested that Amir could advance his career by completing communication workshops, he was interested. Eventually he completed the workshops. Not only did Amir receive an excellent rating in all factors the next time around, he became a tour group supervisor—something that might not have occurred without the formal appraisal interview.

CONCLUSION

Assessment of team members' performance must occur every day. One of the most important responsibilities of a hospitality supervisor is to recognize and respond to performance, be it good or bad. An appraisal without this two-way conference may be in compliance with the procedure, but it is a mockery of its purpose. If your company has a training program on this topic, take advantage of the opportunity and attend. Formal appraisals must evaluate performance against known performance objectives. The two parts to the performance appraisal are content and conference. Appraisals give you an opportunity to use your communication skills. You should apply the five R's of private communications. Constructive feedback on performance is the cornerstone of personal growth and development. Constructive feedback is *not* constructive criticism. A personal performance contract (PPC) is a written document of agreement that establishes future goals for which a team member becomes accountable.

DISCUSSION QUESTIONS

1. Can you explain why many supervisors dread formal reviews? Does their attitude keep them from doing a good job of reviewing? Why is it so difficult to judge or evaluate others?

2. What are the pitfalls of not doing a performance appraisal?

3. Recall the details of your last performance appraisal. How was it handled? What could have been done to improve it and to make it more accurate and beneficial to you?

4. Explain why there should be no surprises in the information shared with the team member in the performance review.

5. How can performance appraisals with your staff help you achieve performance objectives for your area of responsibility?

6. List and explain the four categories for providing constructive feedback.

7. State the reason for establishing a personal performance contract (PPC).

PART V

INCREASING YOUR OWN OPPORTUNITIES

Learning and applying the information presented in the earlier chapters of this book will make you a successful supervisor. In the following chapters we provide you with additional skills for increasing your own opportunities to continue your climb up the hospitality career ladder.

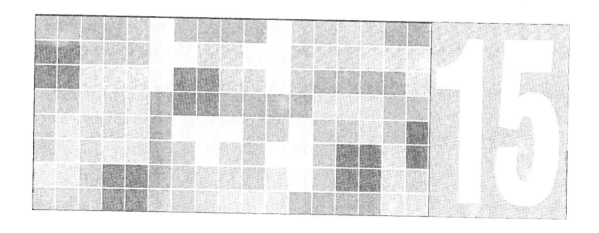

A Positive Workplace Starts with You

I have missed more than 9,000 shots, lost almost 300 games, on 26 occasions been entrusted to take the game winning shot . . . and missed. I have failed over and over again in my life. And that is why I succeed.

–Michael Jordan

After you have finished reading this chapter, you should be able to

- explain how managing your own efforts establishes your success,

- describe how to overcome common challenges that prevent supervisors from being successful,

- list the factors that create a harmonious work environment, and

- describe methods for improving your concentration.

THE SIGNS OF UNSUCCESSFUL SUPERVISION

Most beginning hospitality supervisors discover that their new and demanding responsibilities cause them to move, physically and mentally, in too many directions at the same time. Under these conditions, it is easy to start operating without clear direction. When this sort of behavior occurs, it is a signal that you are not thinking or concentrating enough. The result of such behavior is confusion, frustration, and possibly a drop in productivity.

Take a look at the following list. If these items describe your workplace, you are operating without clear direction.

- Communication impairments exist at all levels.

- Controllables are out of control. Supervisors are working long hours with little results.

- Leadership turnover is high. No loyalty exists between management and the company, and, more critically, between management and team members.

- Supervisors are frustrated and demoralized due to lack of control over the operations.

- Supervisors and team members are seeking employment elsewhere.

- Unit operates in crisis (survival) mode with no clear direction or goals.

Some hospitality supervisors expend a great deal of effort with little achievement. They are very busy, but they aren't making much progress. Often the things on which they are focused and the things they should be doing don't match. In situations like this the supervisor and team members are not equipped to achieve their performance objectives.

Watch for the following signs that you are not equipped to achieve your performance objectives:

- Supervisors and team members lack effective communications. Misunderstandings and operational miscues are common.

SAY HELLO TO MY NEW BURRITO

Fred's first day in the Mexican fast food restaurant served as a wake-up call that his life had changed for the worse. After working ridiculously long hours to successfully turn around a store that was now primed to pay him a bonus, he was transferred here. This restaurant had already seen three general managers. The first general manager had a heart attack. The second had a nervous breakdown. The third walked out on the job.

Upon his arrival, Fred was greeted at the door with hostility: upset customers complaining about how long they had to wait for their food, the quality of food, the unsanitary conditions of the restaurant, and rudeness of the obviously untrained team members. The average ticket time at the drive-through was bordering on 15 minutes and it was climbing. The wait in the dining room was even worse. Fred had heard that previous managers often shut down the dining room and just focused on the drive-through because they could not keep up with the business. Additionally, security personnel were assigned to the unit due to numerous complaints and threats made to previous managers.

Fred no longer wondered why his supervisor did not accompany him to his new restaurant. The most recent audit from corporate told him all that he needed to know. Controllables were out of control, sales were down, and food cost, paper products, and labor were sky high. It also appeared that the store was missing money. With paperwork completely screwed up and at least one deposit "missing," company auditors would be onsite any day now.

Fred wondered if he was being set up. Why did the company send him to this place under these conditions? Already feeling slapped from being moved from his last store, Fred pondered his next move.

- Supervisors and team members are performance oriented, but they are not always doing the right thing, or doing things right.

- Supervisors often have to make do without the necessary tools, training, and time needed to execute the operations effectively and efficiently. They focus on the results and not how the results are achieved.

- A conflict exists over what is expected; supervisors and team members are not operating from the same page. This situation is compounded when more than one supervisor is working in the store and the management team does not agree. Team members working with supervisors in conflict become rigid to change.

- Confusion exists as to what is important. Major focuses are lost among trivial activities.

- There is no continuity from one day to the next. Priorities change on a daily basis, and daily work is performed yielding no long-term value.

- Supervisors rationalize to themselves and their team member that they are doing a better job than they truly are.

> ### PAYROLL IS NOT THE PROBLEM
>
> "We are in on payroll this week," Supervisor Mike excitedly yelled from the grill to Supervisor John, who was washing dishes in the dishroom.
>
> John responded, "Yeah, since we started working team members' positions the last day of payroll each week it's made a difference. It also didn't hurt that we trimmed labor hours on the schedule and we sent people home early every day."
>
> "Once we get labor costs down, we need to focus on increasing sales and customer counts, and doing something about our food cost problem," Mike said.
>
> John yelled, "One problem at a time. Now that we've got this labor thing licked, the other problems are next."

Some hospitality supervisors make the mistake of trying to control every aspect of their operation. In these cases, team members cannot help their supervisors because they are not authorized to act on their own. This situation usually occurs because the supervisor is still trying to learn the job and learn how to execute his or her responsibilities.

The following signals may suggest that you are experiencing this problem:

- Challenges in the work place are resolved quickly but not always effectively. Ownership of responsibility often exhibits a "pass the buck" mentality.

- Management concerns about making mistakes stifle creativity. Playing it safe becomes the motto of operations.

- Supervisors avoid the risk of making decisions. Issues at the local level are kicked up to upper management.

- Supervisors fail to delegate nonmanagement duties to other personnel; they are getting results by being warrior supervisors.

- Personnel members are told to take charge, but they lack the authority to carry out their duties.

- Personnel skills are limited due to lack of cross training. Supervisors have tunnel vision and do not utilize team members beyond their primary positions.

- Team members know what needs to be done but don't always do it until they are told when and how to perform. Team members have the attitude that they are not paid to think.

CREATING A HARMONIOUS WORK ENVIRONMENT

Some hospitality supervisors invest their time and energy in establishing a foundation that allows them great success. They have learned how to share their vision and expectations in the workplace. They are willing to work hard to put the systems in place and instill the proper work habits of team members to yield the results they expect. Team members are working in partnership with the operation, and the expectations of the supervisor and the team members are in harmony.

WAITING DO BE TOLD	
Server Team Member to Kitchen Team Member:	"You better start baking some potatoes. We're going to need some for the dinner rush."
Kitchen Team Member to Server Team Member:	"I know we are going to run out, but the last time I put some potatoes in the oven without being told I got yelled at. I know when we need to cook them, but I am not doing anything until I am told."
Supervisor to Customer:	"Sorry we ran out of baked potatoes. Our food guide said we only needed three pans. I am waiting on corporate to fix the guide so that we don't run out. Here's your refund."
Customer to Supervisor:	"It will be great once they work out the kinks. I have been here three times. Two times in a row you ran out of baked potatoes."

The following elements are needed for a positive workplace:

- *Clear direction and vision.* Everyone (supervisor and team members) knows the plan and how to achieve it.

- *Effective leadership.* The supervisor is working with team members to elevate their performance by providing training, materials, and time to team members. The supervisor is focused on educating, enabling, and empowering his or her team members' abilities.

- *Excellent communications.* Everyone is on the same page; communication flows up and down the chain of command.

- *Tools and resources.* Although mindful of controllables, there are ample resources available to effectively perform every job.

- *Supervisors and team members work together to accomplish the work.* They are performing the right things the right way. They are motivated to work to the best of their abilities, and they work with a sense of pride and ownership in the operation.

Making Positive Change

To have the success you deserve, you have to work on the first team member in your store that you can change—yourself.

Improving Your Focus

Concentration is being able to focus your mental attention on a chosen project while you temporarily ignore matters of less importance. It means devoting your mind exclusively to one problem until you have the best solution you are capable of reaching. (Concentration is also getting the full message from a chapter you are reading!) The nice thing about concentration is that it is a mental discipline anyone can learn.

Eliminating Distractions

To accomplish a job that involves thinking, it is often necessary to isolate yourself from the many distractions most front-line supervisors face. These distractions include interruptions from team members, customers, and superiors; emergency problems; repair tasks; paperwork; filling in for an absent team member; and, of course, the telephone.

> Frieda makes it a practice to arrive at her desk 30 minutes ahead of her team members each morning. "I need to get away from telephone calls, team member interruptions, and normal noise to improve my concentration. Thirty minutes before the gang arrives is worth an hour when the shift is under way."

> George, an audio-video supervisor, stays on site for an hour or so after everyone else has left. "I need some quiet time to plan for the next day. I concentrate on having all the supplies ready for the crew when they arrive so that we can get off to a fast start. And, of course, it is a mistake to read service contracts unless you have 100% concentration."

> Hank has found a park bench near his noisy office where only the birds and the breeze can be heard. "When I have a knotty problem or need to concentrate on a report that is due, I often take my briefcase and head for my second office. On rainy days, I simply wait until I get home that night."

> Isabelle divides her job as a supervisor into two categories. "First, I have my work time, which is devoted to tasks, counseling team members, keeping everyone informed, and making routine decisions. Then I have my mind-time responsibilities, which include doing work schedules, setting goals, making big decisions, and doing some creative thinking. Work time (90%) occurs under all kinds of conditions; mind time occurs when I step back to a quiet place where I can view the operation from a distance."

> Samantha comes in a half an hour early and stays a half an hour late everyday. "What I do before the shift begins and after the shift has ended makes me more successful everyday. I have time to think about the day ahead and recap my challenges and accomplishments daily."

Concentrating to Learn versus Concentrating to Manage

Anyone can improve his or her power of concentration. Those with college degrees have obviously had opportunities to increase this power by mastering study habits and techniques. This practice gives them a slight advantage, but there is a big difference between concentrating to learn and concentrating to solve real work problems. Supervisors have so many immediate tasks to perform that when they concentrate on a major problem they must walk away, quickly concentrate, and then return to the remaining tasks. They do not have the luxury of sitting in a library where the environment is conducive to concentration.

People who have trained their minds to do analytical thinking—especially when numbers and formulas are involved—seem to have the edge when deep concentration is required. These same people are often good at goal setting and planning because they like to figure things out. This ability does not mean, however, that those with a different background cannot learn to concentrate at a high enough level to be effective. All it takes is practice and a few simple rules.

> When Martin accepted the position of supervisor with a chain restaurant, he didn't fully realize how much planning would be involved. A high school dropout, Martin never focused his mind on anything for more than a few moments. How would he survive? His supervisor told him to isolate himself for 30 minutes each work day and do nothing but develop a written priority list of duties to perform that day. Slowly, through mental discipline, Martin learned to plan ahead. Along the way, he also learned to concentrate in other areas.

Barriers to Concentration.   In this hectic field of work, it is never easy to take time away from other responsibilities in order to concentrate on a special project. Many barriers keep supervisors from being able to concentrate. Some of these barriers are physical; others are psychological. Check those in the following list that frequently keep you from concentrating.

- Telephone calls

- Interruptions by team members or co-workers

- Noise

- Preoccupation on another matter

- Lack of training in how to concentrate

- Low tolerance of frustration

- Lack of motivation

- Procrastination

- Fatigue or stress

- A "to-heck-with-it" attitude

Due to many factors, particularly the influence of individual personalities, some people find it easier to concentrate than others. Some actually enjoy the process. Bill and Hazel provide us with an excellent example.

> Bill and Hazel operate a successful reception rental company. You seldom see Bill because he is in the back office, thinking through problems and planning ahead. His training as an engineer and computer programmer has given him unusual powers of concentration that fit his quiet personality. Hazel, on the other hand, works out front doing a superior job with customers. She loves people and makes the most of her outgoing personality. Obviously, the division of work between Hazel and Bill is ideal. Last year, Bill had open heart surgery and Hazel found it necessary to take over his work in addition to doing her own. By the time Bill returned, things were a mess. "What did you expect?" said Hazel. "I can't deal effectively with demanding customers and concentrate at the same time."

Few supervisors are fortunate enough to have another person to do their concentrating. Most must wear two hats. One is used to deal with daily operational tasks (working with customers, dealing with production factors, etc.), and the other is used for planning purposes. With desire and training, Hazel, in our previous example, could learn to do both, as is the case with almost all supervisors.

Tips on How to Concentrate.   In assuming your responsibilities as a new supervisor, learning to wear both hats effectively is important. Here are a few tips that will assist you in switching to concentration mode.

- *Limit your time.* It is not how much time you spend concentrating that is important, but how intensely your mind is focused while you are at it. Experience shows that when you limit yourself to a certain amount of time for concentration purposes (say, 30 minutes instead of an hour), you accomplish more.

  > Matt, a supervisor in a commissary, has a difficult report due each Friday morning. For years he has devoted a full afternoon on Thursday to completing the report. Then he discovered that if he allocated only two hours each Thursday afternoon (always in a quiet front office where no one could reach him), he could complete the report in half the time with fewer mistakes. In discussing this change with his supervisor, Matt said, "Apparently, when I limit my time, I concentrate better."

- *Divide and conquer big projects.* When facing a major project like preparing an annual report or budget, it is often a good idea to divide the work into smaller parts. Short, intense periods of concentration make more sense than trying to concentrate for an extended period of time when mental fatigue can set in.

  > Sylvia wanted to write an orientation manual for her corporation, but every time she sat down to put her thoughts in order, an interruption occurred and she would become frustrated and give up. Then, with permission from her supervisor, she tried a different approach. She left work early each Friday afternoon and went straight home, where she devoted two solid hours of concentration to the project. By spreading out the work, Sylvia was able to complete it in six weeks. Her supervisor was most complimentary when she turned in the finished project.

- *Visualize the benefits.* Concentration is aided when the rewards that come from a completed project are pictured in advance. Such visualization can increase motivation.

  > When Polly's divorce was final, she had to decide whether to do her own income tax or pay a professional. To keep expenses down, Polly decided to do it herself. To provide motivation, she pictured herself on a skiing trip with the money she would save. Always good with figures, she discovered she enjoyed the process because it gave her a better view of where her limited income was going. It also gave her an annual ski trip.

- *Project a professional image.* Supervisors who learn to concentrate on setting goals, establishing priorities, and completing special projects communicate a more professional image to upper management. They demonstrate that they can come through when clear thinking and decision making are necessary.

Roberto had the reputation of being a happy-go-lucky supervisor who got the job done but was not interested in a higher position. When he turned 30, Roberto decided to go back to finish his college degree so that he could give his career a boost. In doing so, he learned how to concentrate, and after he submitted a few new projects, management took a second look at Roberto as middle management material.

■ *Getting it done.* Procrastination is the postponement of an important project without a good reason. It is, in effect, backing away from the periods of concentration necessary to get something accomplished.

> Raymond discovered that self-talk was his best method to get into a mood in which he could concentrate. He would say to himself: "Here you go again, backing away because you are too lazy to concentrate. Get it done now so that you will feel better this weekend."

Eight Steps to Success

The next time you need to concentrate on a major problem or project, follow these simple steps:

1. **Isolate yourself.** Find a location where you are free from interruptions and excessive noise. Once you arrive, make yourself comfortable. Relax enough so that other matters leave your mind. You are then ready to concentrate.

2. **Review the situation.** If you are concentrating with the help of a computer, bring up all facts and past history. If you are working away from a computer, have all available data with you, including printouts. Study the data.

3. **Give yourself a time limit.** With full concentration, 15 minutes is a long time. Attempt to beat the time allotments you have used in similar situations in the past.

4. **Outline what you intend to do and get started.** Most people think better with a pencil in hand.

5. **List all options.** Review the various possibilities and strategies that might improve the situation or solve the problem. Ask for help from your peers and employees when needed.

6. **Weigh and decide.** Thinking means tossing possibilities back and forth in your mind until you come up with the best approach or solution.

7. **Make a decision or complete the project.** Whatever has required your concentration now needs to be implemented or stored in your memory bank for future use. Concentration almost always produces something of value.

8. **When you find yourself procrastinating on an important project, take action.** Organize your day to allow some period of time for the project and work on it for the entire time allotted. Just do it! As they say, "The job never started takes the longest to finish."

CONCLUSION

Most beginning hospitality supervisors discover that their new and demanding responsibilities cause them to move, physically and mentally, in too many directions at the same time. Under these conditions, it is easy to start operating without clear direction.

Hospitality supervisors may make the mistake of trying to control every aspect of their operation. In these cases, team members cannot help their supervisors because they are not authorized to act on their own.

Productive supervisors have learned how to share their vision and expectations in the workplace. They are willing to work hard to put the systems in place and instill the proper work habits of team members to yield the results they expect. Team members are working in partnership with the operation and the expectations of the supervisor and the team members are in harmony.

Concentration is being able to focus your mental attention on a chosen project while you temporarily ignore matters of less importance. Anyone can improve his or her power of concentration.

DISCUSSION QUESTIONS

1. In "Say Hello to My New Burrito," what challenges did Fred encounter? How would you manage this situation if you were Fred?

2. In "Payroll Is Not the Problem," how did supervisors Mike and John lie to themselves that they are making progress? What are the real issues with their operations? How is their labor solution creating more problems for their operations?

3. In "Refunds after Refunds," what is really holding back the operation?

4. What are your barriers to concentration? How can you overcome these barriers?

5. Apply the Eight Steps to Success to a problem/project. Explain each step.

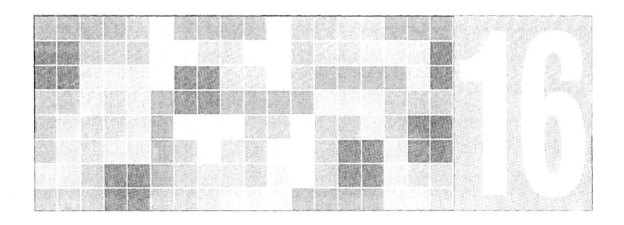

Organization
and Planning

What would you attempt to do if you knew you could not fail?

–Dr. Robert Schuller

After you have finished reading this chapter, you should be able to

- write an operations plan in detail and adapt it to your own work situation,

- explain the tools you can use to develop daily and weekly goals,

- describe the characteristics of a successful operations plan, and

- discuss the importance of having computer skills in the hospitality industry.

PLANNING: ESTABLISHING GOALS AND OBJECTIVES

"I prefer not to be a supervisor. Sure I'd like the salary but no amount of money is worth the headaches that comes with trying to control this whole department. I'd rather be able to show up, do my job and leave when my shift is over. My supervisor shows up early to get things organized and then takes work home with her in the evening. No sir, I don't want that. Let the supervisor do the planning, scheduling, and have the worries of making everyone productive."

This quotation may not express the best possible team member attitude, but it brings up some important issues. If the supervisor doesn't give the unit direction, who will? If she or he doesn't organize, plan, schedule, and pick up the loose ends, where will such leadership come from? If the supervisor does not set goals and form plans to make sure they are carried out on time and within their budget, who will?

Some fairly basic differences separate the positions of team member and supervisor. The team member can become involved in the activities of the department without worrying over where the department is going. He or she can achieve job satisfaction without sweating out reports, plans, figures, purchases, statistics, comparisons, and so forth. The supervisor, on the other hand, must constantly look at the overall picture. Are all team members properly assigned and fully productive? How is the operation doing compared to other operations? How much increase in productivity might be expected in the next six months? What cost factors can be eliminated or reduced?

It is important to understand the differences between goals and objectives. Often the terms are used as though they were the same things. But they are different. Goals are broad statements that identify something an organization wishes to achieve or accomplish. For example, a goal may be to increase companywide productivity by 10% annually. An objective, on the other hand, is a very specific action taken to achieve the stated goal. Providing supervisors with training in organizational skills is an example of an objective. Accomplishing this training objective moves the organization toward its goal of increasing productivity. The more the objective supports goal achievement, the better.

PLANS MEAN CHANGE

If you want to make a change you need a plan. If you want things to stay as they are, you need a policy. Change of any kind, large or small, needs a plan to make it happen. A wise person once said, "A goal is a dream with a deadline." So true! Setting a goal is the first step in achieving the goal. To illustrate, let us say that you are at Point A. Point A is the actual state of affairs where you are at present. Let us say that you decide that Point A is no longer satisfactory and you wish to make changes. Think of the changes as a journey from Point A to Point B. Point B is the target, the desired state of affairs, how you want things to be. Point B becomes your goal.

The actions you take to move to Point B become your objectives. Getting to a goal may take many objectives. Those things that impede your progress to the goal are called obstacles.

Reaching goals often involves overcoming tough obstacles. It certainly includes planning. Planning is essential to reaching almost every goal. Few people would go on a vacation without planning it in advance. Decisions about where to go, how to get there, how long to stay, how much money to take, and what clothing to pack are but a few of the important decisions to make before going. Planning is especially important if you take someone with you. Before leaving Point A, the person may want detailed information or more. Taking that first step on a 1000-mile journey is an objective; so is taking the last step. The better the planning, the more likely the goal will be achieved.

The successful supervisor realizes that when a change is likely to affect the work or routine of team members, the team members should be involved in the planning stage of the change. Too often those most affected by a change are only involved in the implementation stage of the change and not in the planning stage. Team members may resist change because they were not involved in the planning stage. If you desire to move your team members to Point B, to the desired state, you will need their motivation and cooperation to move, to change. An effective way to encourage this motivation is through involvement in planning

ORGANIZATION-LEVEL GOALS: THE BIG PICTURE

Supervisors cannot just let things happen; they must make them happen. They must control a multitude of factors, deal with countless emergencies, and pick up a variety of loose ends, constantly directing and guiding the activities of others. No matter how many details must be faced, no matter how frantic the pace, supervisors are expected to stay on top of the situation and be in control. Very few people like to work in an unorganized environment. How can the supervisor do all these things? By being an organized person with a definite plan.

Leaders must occasionally elevate their thinking high above the trees so that they can see the forest. They must learn how to plan so that they can achieve significant, appropriate, and practical goals. The degree to which a supervisor is successful in seeing the big picture will determine the long-range success that he or she will enjoy. The big picture takes form and clarity when the supervisor is able to explain how his or her department contributes to the goals and objectives of the entire company. This means that supervisors are well aware of the goals and objectives of their organization and plan work that enhances the possibility of achieving those goals. This knowledge should come from being involved in the planning and formulation of organization-level goals.

All supervisory planning should start by identifying organization-level goals. These are the broad goals of the company that are usually stated in the strategic plan, in team member handbooks, or in annual reports to stockholders. Goals are expressed in terms of service standards, sales volume, customer counts, profit pictures, or similar criteria. Goals will change from time to time. It is best when supervisors have direct input in forming goals. It is the responsibility of supervisors to relate the operation of the unit to the established goals. To do so, the supervisor should develop and operation-level plan for his or her department. Begin by asking these questions:

1. What are the current goals of my company?

2. How might my operation contribute to reaching these goals?

3. Is my operation doing anything not in conformity with these goals?

Goals are often related to organizational values. What does your organization value? What are the important things? Identifying what your organization measures will reveal its values. For example, if your hotel measures customer satisfaction on cleanliness, the management of the hotel values customer satisfaction and cleanliness. Identifying the values of your organization and planning and organizing work to enhance these values is a recipe for success.

OPERATION-LEVEL PLANNING

You should develop your own operations plan geared toward the broad goals and then communicate it to your own team members.

Operations plans can take many forms, so you may receive considerable help from your boss in building your plan. He or she may ask you for a monthly, semi-annual, or yearly written plan; provide the necessary forms; and give you a model to work from. On the other hand, if your supervisor does not ask you for a plan, you may prepare one exclusively for your own purposes. In either case, you should do the following:

■ Make your plan workable because an impossible goal does not motivate.

■ Make your plan flexible so that you can adjust to changes beyond your control.

■ Include all elements or factors over which you have control.

■ State the expected increase in productivity (tangible, sales, or service) in clear terms. Always include previous figures for comparison.

■ Tie your plan to organization-level goals.

■ Involve your team members in formulating your objectives.

A workable operations plan is not easy to develop. It will take time, effort, and some communication on your part, but without a plan you lack direction. The kind of plan you develop will depend on many variables. Try to involve your team members in the formulation of the plan because they will be expected to help accomplish it. It is human nature for people to be motivated to carry out plans they have had a part in creating.

Let's assume that you have developed an operations plan. It contains the broad objectives you hope to reach in your operations in the next six months or year. It states the things you hope to achieve so that your department will show growth and improvement and will make its maximum contribution to the organization as a whole.

If you can accomplish these goals or come close to them, your reputation as a supervisor will be greatly enhanced. Once you set these goals, you have committed yourself. Make adjustments when necessary, make new ones as things change, but stick to the objectives and to the plan.

Short-Term Goals

You cannot, of course, reach the goals of your overall plan unless you make it work by dividing it into smaller objectives that are achievable on a daily or weekly basis. Many experienced supervisors develop a daily checklist (tied to operations plans), which they follow as closely as the situation permits.

> "While driving to work in the morning, I organize my day by making up a list of things to do. When I get to my desk, I write this list on my calendar pad and assign priorities. I then spend the rest of the day trying to check them off. It works for me."

> "I never leave work, even if I'm late, until I have a priority list of things to do when I show up the next day. This list makes it easier for me to leave my problems at work and gives me a good starting point the next day. I'd recommend it to the beginning supervisor."

> "For the last 20 years, I've made it a practice to show up 15 minutes early every morning so that I can organize my daily plan. I find I can sort things out more clearly this time of day."

Small daily plans eventually add up to the successful completion of overall operations plans. The daily checklist is an excellent practice and is strongly recommended for both the new and the experienced supervisor. The key to such a list is setting up the right priorities and following certain rules. It must be emphasized, however, that the only worthwhile goals are reachable goals. Some supervisors divide their small plans into daily and weekly classifications. A weekly goal might include something that takes more than one day to accomplish, such as changing a basic procedure, training a new team member, or contacting a series of customers. A daily goal might include taking care of customers, recognizing a team member, completing paperwork, or similar activities.

Use a Calendar

Effective managers who set project deadlines for themselves use calendars. Deadlines act as reminders and facilitate productivity. Calendars also can be used for planning sales promotions, booking parties, and scheduling staff meetings and training. Some managers prefer large calendars that can be displayed in their office as a reminder to all staff members. Others prefer pocket varieties that can be used both at home and on the job. No matter what type of calendar you use, make sure you use one. Beginning supervisors do not need highly complex systems to handle their responsibilities, but they can benefit from a simple one.

DEPARTMENT SUCCESS

Department success in reaching goals and objectives is a combination of many factors, but being an organized person is certainly one of them. This is especially true of supervisors because only those who can organize a small department can organize a larger operation. The sooner you demonstrate to your superiors that you have the ability to organize yourself and your department, the sooner you will start your climb up the career ladder.

Angie is a coffee house manager. She has been charged with the responsibility of opening up a new restaurant in an enclosed shopping center. How might she approach this assignment?

Angie wants her operation to achieve four basic goals.

1. to control overhead expense,
2. to grow the unit's profitability,
3. to market the image of the coffee house through a higher quality of service, and
4. to establish a cultural mix of team members and bring more women into management.

Angie feels strongly that her small branch (only 15 team members) can contribute to these companywide objectives.

A few weeks before she opened her coffee house, Angie was required to submit a plan for the first six months of operation. It was based to some extent on what other new coffee houses of the same size and in similar situations had experienced. It included the following:

1. the date she anticipated the operation would become profitable;
2. sales and customer count figures she hoped to achieve, stated monthly; and
3. a customer service plan that she hoped would satisfy all clients, especially those business organizations in the shopping center that would depend heavily on her services.

Angie has her own system when it comes to small-action plans or goals. Each weekend (usually at home) she develops a few weekly goals. She writes them in her appointment notebook. They include goals such as:

1. developing special promotional efforts to build clientele,
2. getting reports to the corporate office in better shape and before deadlines,

3. planning a short staff meeting, and

4. performing a performance appraisal that needs to be done.

But Angie does not let it go at that; she also uses a daily goal system. Every morning when she arrives and opens the coffee shop, she takes 10 minutes to sit down and write on her desk calendar the smaller things she wants to accomplish before she goes home. Often there are deadlines for these priorities. Some of these goals she has thought about on the way to work, so it only takes a few minutes to write them down. She may add one or two during the day, but she makes an effort to check them off as she goes. Again, this activity is a private matter. On days when she completes all her small goals, she has a great sense of satisfaction. Sometimes, of course, she must postpone a few goals until the next day because a hectic pace prevented her from attending to them.

Here are some tips that will help you get started on organizing your daily and weekly goals:

- *Involve your team members.* Participation in planning enhances the motivation of those who are expected to carry out the plan.

- *Keep your operations plans simple.* An operations plan is simply a proposed blueprint, or map, for the future. An ultra-sophisticated plan may look pretty, but it may not be workable. Keep it simple and attainable.

- *Organize yourself on a daily basis.* Most supervisors need a simple procedure to follow each day in order to accomplish first things first and follow through on other activities. The daily checklist is a worthwhile tool.

- *Achieve results through people.* Your operations plan and your daily checklist are useless unless you put them into action through people. You must develop your human relations skills to make your plan work.

- *Be a do-it-yourself goal setter.* Seek opportunities through analysis of your operation to discover ways to improve it. Identify, refine, and implement ideas to make improvements.

- *Be assertive.* Assert yourself by creating objectives for your unit. Do not wait for your supervisor to encourage you. Communicate that you are already an organized person with an upper management future.

USING TECHNOLOGY

Today, all employees at every level need to be computer literate. This is especially true for supervisors. Supervisors who fail to learn computer systems or take advantage of management information systems (MISs) will find themselves on the outside looking in.

Computerized information systems are reshaping many organizations. Traditional operations boundaries are giving way to information networks. Computers facilitate decentralization in organizations with little or no loss of control. The pace of business leaves no room for debate. The supervisor who does not develop strong computer skills is heavily handicapped and will eventually lose out to those who do. Fortunately, most future supervisors are already computer literate. Later, as they move into higher management, they are likely to find themselves traveling on an airplane using a laptop computer with access to messages and information anytime, anywhere. Computers are an indispensable tool in the supervisor's survival kit.

Software

To illustrate how the supervisor of the future can make maximum use of the computer, all we need to do is review the basic software packages currently available.

Document programs: Word processing allows a busy supervisor to be his or her own secretary. For example, a bulletin may need to be written (with graphics), edited, and posted in a hurry. No problem with a word processor.

Spreadsheets: This software allows the supervisor to turn the computer's memory into a large worksheet in which data formulas can be tested. For example, a supervisor may want to discover what hiring a new team member would do to profitability. A few moments on the computer and the answer is on the screen.

Database management: These programs make it possible to obtain and review information from a larger base to make comparisons.

Graphics: These programs display information in the form of charts or graphs that can be used in short operations meetings and other forms of communication.

Networking: Programs that interface permit the transfer of data to and from other supervisors and managers. The impact of networking on interorganizational communications is already being felt.

Most companies will have customized computer programs to manage their operation. Having a working knowledge of computer and program applications can reduce the learning time in mastering company systems.

CONCLUSION

Planning and organizing are essential skills for the effective supervisor. An effective plan contains goals and objectives. Goals and objectives are two different things. Establishing specific objectives that support goal achievement is essential to success. Participation in planning goals and objectives enhances motivation in those expected to carry out the objectives. The computer is a very important tool that can increase your productivity and effectiveness in planning and organizing. Learn how to use the computer software that affects your operations.

DISCUSSION QUESTIONS

1. Do you agree that when supervisors prepare their own written plans (with little or no pressure from management), they are more likely to translate the plan into motivating goals? Why or why not?

2. In what ways will an organized plan affect the productivity of your team members?

3. How might you involve your team members in the planning and organization of an operation plan?

4. What effect does participation in planning have on motivation?

5. Could a supervisor overplan (i.e., be too concerned about what is to be done when and by whom)? What effect could overplanning have on team members' productivity?

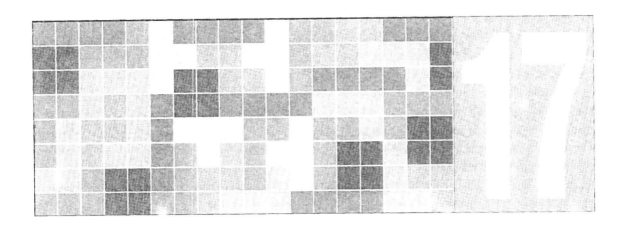

Setting Priorities

"I'll do it tomorrow."—Everyone

After you have finished reading this chapter, you should be able to

- describe how to improve your ability to prioritize,

- define the ABC method of prioritizing,

- discuss the advantages of keeping a written priority list, and

- describe ways to manage your time better.

Priorities are a vital part of any plan. In one respect, they are the plan. They indicate what you feel is most important and what can be ignored temporarily. Obviously, people who are good at setting priorities accomplish their plans or goals more easily and efficiently than those who are not.

In putting a plan into operation, you need to concentrate on doing the most urgent tasks first. A particular task does not need to be handled first just because it is assigned to you first, and just because you didn't have time to do something yesterday does not mean it should have top priority today.

Many benefits come from setting goals and priorities, including the following:

- *Achieving more.* You become more organized in your work. By prioritizing your activities, you can give more attention to getting the important things done first and you have more energy to devote to your work because your efforts are focused.

- *Improving productivity.* One sets a goal because the current state of affairs needs to change. If current productivity levels need to improve, specific productivity goals can help to reach the desired level.

- *Improving self-confidence.* Reaching goals builds self-confidence, and self-confidence promotes growth and personal development. As you achieve goals, you also becomes less fearful of risk taking. Resistance to change may be a byproduct of such fears; setting goals and formulating a plan helps to overcome them. The confidence your team members have in you as their leader also will improve as your goals become reality, especially when they benefit directly from the goal.

- *Communicating more clearly.* An effective goal is precise, has set priorities, and is documented. It communicates to everyone where they are headed.

- *Limiting procrastination.* Deadlines or due dates cause things to happen; they are control measures. Procrastination may result from unspecified due dates rather than lack of motivation on the part of those the changes affect. Target dates for things help to move activity toward goal accomplishment.

- *Reducing stress.* Accomplishing goals may reduce your stress because you have the realization that you are in control and organized. Distress and depression may come from dwelling on unrealized goals.

IDENTIFY AND PRIORITIZE TASKS

Identifying tasks and setting priorities is a skill that you can get better at doing the more you do it. The key to effective prioritizing is having the ability to rank order tasks according to their importance and relevance to the goal you wish to reach—putting "first things first," as it were. One tool to place in your survival kit is the following two-step process for prioritizing. Using this process will enhance your ability to reach your goals by effectively prioritizing goal-related tasks.

Two-Step Process for Prioritizing

Step 1: Identify all the tasks that need to be accomplished in reaching the goal. A good way to do this is involve your team members in the process. Remember that many heads are better than one. Communicate the goal to them and then use their input to determine what needs to be done to accomplish the goal. List all the tasks in a written form in the file.

Step 2: Prioritize or rank order the list of tasks using the ABC method.

- Priority A includes "must do" items that are critical.
- Priority B is "should do" items without critical deadlines.
- Priority C constitutes "fun to do" or "when I have time" tasks that can usually be saved for slack periods.

Ask these eight questions when deciding what tasks to put in which category. Involve your team members in completing this step.

1. If I deal with this problem first, will it automatically solve others later?
2. If I deal with this problem first, will it delay the solution of another that will eventually cause severe damage to productivity or my career?
3. If I delay action on this problem, will it solve itself?
4. What can I delegate so that I can get to more serious problems sooner?
5. Will taking care of this small problem first free my mind to take care of my number one problem later?
6. What tasks must I complete quickly so that I will not hold up the schedule of other people or other departments?
7. Can I group a few things together and save time by solving them all at once?
8. Is the time psychologically right to take up a problem with my boss, or should I wait for a more appropriate time?

As you work with the process of setting priorities you will realize how complex and demanding it can be and that it will never be perfect. Yet the more effective you become, the more success you can anticipate. Many supervisors have learned that keeping a written list of priorities is best. The list may need constant revision due to changes occurring in the work environment.

Criteria for Setting Priorities

Experts describe three basic yardsticks to follow in setting priorities:

1. **Judgment.** You may be the best judge of your situation, but prioritizing is not always a do-it-yourself undertaking. Involve others.

2. **Relativity.** Relativity can best be determined by asking the question, "What is the best use of my time right now?" When you are not making the most of your time, you are paying the opportunity cost. Opportunity cost is the price you pay for doing things that are not the best use of your time.

3. **Timing.** Deadlines often dictate priorities, but starting times need to be made in advance, and these decisions involve the priority process.

Advantages of a Written List

You may have the aptitude to keep a running priority list in your mind, but most beginning supervisors find it advantageous to write a list on a desk pad for the following reasons:

1. Writing the list is a form of self-discipline. When you know what needs to be done next, you are organized and less likely to waste time.

2. The list frequently eliminates forgetting, which can get you in trouble with your supervisor. Some supervisors simply prefer to trust visible lists instead of their memories.

3. Completing a list and checking off items is satisfying and motivating. A priority list is, in effect, a personal reward system.

Keeping Priority Lists Flexible

The first thing you learn about setting priorities is that the order may not last long. All it takes is a call from your supervisor, an emergency situation, an unexpected human relations problem, or a mechanical breakdown to force you to make up a new list.

A priority list is not a static thing and may need revision many times a day. In fact, many supervisors automatically reevaluate their priorities every time they move from one completed task to another. Then, you may ask, why make a list in the first place? The primary reason is to keep all responsibilities, tasks, and problems in view. A priority list should include all tasks that need to be done to reach your goals as soon as possible.

Obviously, it would be a serious mistake to leave something off the list that should be on it. Even if your list is complete, however, you can still make mistakes by putting one task or problem ahead of another. For example, if you spend your time on what should be a lower-priority matter, you are neglecting something more crucial, and this can result in more harm than good. To illustrate the importance of this concept, look at the following examples:

Sid is a supervisor for a four diamond hotel. Last week it was announced that the hotel would have an announced inspection by a team of top management. Sid wanted a good report so badly that he gave top priority to cleaning up and rearranging the department. Everything else was neglected. Predictably, Sid and the department received a 100% rating. But what happened to the other priorities? For one thing, Sid neglected to turn in a computerized merchandise reorder list on time and the department was out of stock for two weeks. Sid—and his department—paid a high price for a poor priority decision.

Gayle was so fed up with the poorly organized files in her department that she finally decided to reorganize them herself, making it her top priority. Once she got into the task, she discovered that things were worse and took much longer than she anticipated. As a result, she neglected other important matters, including annual reviews of the six people in her department. Her supervisor was upset about it. Later, as Gayle thought it over, she realized that if she had taken care of the reviews first, she could have used them to motivate her team members to clean up the files themselves. She permitted her frustration to overemphasize one problem at the expense of another that should have been first priority.

Effective Priority Setting

How can you set priorities that will make it easier for you to reach your goals and keep you out of trouble? Here are some suggestions:

- *Give priority to any problem that is rendering you ineffective as a supervisor.* Sometimes an upsetting human relations problem might be bothering you, such as a conflict with one of your team members or a serious communications conflict with your supervisor. Such situations can disturb you emotionally and make you ineffective, or at least not up to standard in the rest of your work.

- *Do not focus only on your top-priority task.* Frequently supervisors become so involved in reaching one goal that they neglect others, resulting in more harm in the long run. Keep all your priorities in mind and balance them to prevent shortsightedness.

- *Sometimes it is good to delay a problem or task, giving it a lower priority.* Some problems become so complicated that an immediate solution is impossible. More time is needed to evaluate the facts and measure the total impact. In such instances, you might wish to drop the problem to the bottom of your list, where you can watch it but not forget it.

- *Sometimes you can group goals into a meaningful sequence.* Many supervisors are good at putting their daily goals into a priority pattern that saves time and effort. Examples include making one trip to accomplish three goals or arranging tasks in sequence so that they are easier to accomplish.

- *If something has been on your list for a long time, either do it or forget it.* An item that keeps showing up on a priority list soon becomes an irritant. Do not give it that power.

- *Do not push what should be a high-priority item to the bottom of your list because of fear.* Some managers keep what should be top-priority items undercover because they are afraid to face them. This kind of denial is a serious mistake because time solves very few problems.

■ *Don't oscillate back and forth from one priority to another.* Once you put a task near the top of your list, try to complete it within a reasonable period of time. If you start something and then keep switching to another priority, you will lose all motivation to complete the first project.

Getting Started

If setting up a priority list is a new experience for you, the following tips will help you get started. Later, after you have had additional experience, you can adapt the process to your own style. If you are not currently a supervisor, you may wish to set up a personal priority list as a practice exercise.

1. Select the task or project that will, in your opinion, advance the productivity of your department the most and put it at the top of your list. Leave it there until it is completed or a more important task surfaces.

2. List two additional tasks or projects that are less important but should still be numbered 2 and 3 on your pad. Frequently these tasks present less time pressure.

3. List, in succession, any tasks (reports, appointments, telephone calls, counseling) that either must or should be accomplished before you leave work.

4. Select and list a "fun" project—something you can look forward to doing as an end-of-day personal reward—near or at the bottom of your list.

5. Try to restrict the number of tasks on your list to about seven. Too many priority projects can lead to confusion and a decrease in motivation. Even though it may be your goal to accomplish as much as possible in a single day, some tasks will wait until tomorrow. Those who overschedule themselves take the risk of turning out poor-quality work with higher levels of frustration.

Check off the items on your priority list and prepare a new one at the end of the day. You will transfer some unfinished tasks to the new list, realign them, and add new ones. This process accomplishes two psychological goals. First, it helps you leave your responsibilities at work so you will be free to enjoy your leisure time. Second, arriving at work the following day with a prepared list saves time and can be self-motivating.

Setting priorities for personal tasks off the job can be as important as those at work. If you use what you have learned in this chapter in both environments, you will automatically do a better job of balancing home and career.

BEGINNING THE DAY WITH A GAME PLAN

If you establish sound goals for your operations and yourself and learn to set priorities on a daily basis, will you automatically become more effective at managing your time? Not necessarily. You still need to deal with the basic problem of time allocation itself.

Why should you make a special effort to manage your time? Recent discussions with successful managers indicate that those who arrive at work with a plan for success accomplish the following:

■ Improve productivity attitudes when they greet staff arrivals with an upbeat message or compliment to start the day.

■ Do a better job of organizing their day.

■ Set a better example for their team members.

■ Are less frustrated and have less stress.

A good supervisor senses and handles problems before they get out of hand. When you learn to manage your time well, you can prevent fires rather than spending your time putting them out. Because you are on top of your job—not always catching up—productivity is more even, fewer emergencies and unpleasant surprises emerge, and you have fewer problems to handle.

Until you learn to organize and manage your time well enough to take on additional responsibilities, you are not promotable.

■ You cannot prepare for the next position if you are bogged down in your present job.

■ You cannot do a good job of personal career development if you habitually operate on a crisis basis.

■ You must make more time now through better time management to prepare for a bigger role in the future.

HOW TO MANAGE YOUR TIME

Frank is a successful, highly respected district manager of Ten Day Traders Sandwich Shops. He has time to play racquetball each day, never neglects his family, devotes time to his church, takes care of personal business matters, and still has time left over for social and personal leisure activities. How does he do it? Frank manages his time.

Frank didn't always manage his time wisely. He learned to value his on-the-job time more fully. For a long time he didn't worry how long it took him to do things, but then he suddenly realized he was spending more hours than necessary on certain assignments. As a matter of fact, he was spending more time than was necessary on the job itself and it was beginning to encroach on his leisure time and influence his lifestyle. Frank soon realized that time was one thing he couldn't stretch. He was expected to complete his work in eight hours. If he didn't, it was his fault, not the job's or the company's. The only alternative to better time management was to dip into his personal time. It was then that he decided that his time could be managed better. Know what he discovered? If you learn to manage your working hours, you seem to enjoy your nonworking hours more.

There are several ways to manage your work time more effectively. Some suggestions follow:

1. **Delegate more.** The best way to save your own time is to let somebody else do the task. Many managers could save far more time than they think if they delegated more effectively. Nothing is more time consuming than having an overworked supervisor with underworked team members. Yet it happens frequently.

   > Every morning John rushes to open the store while his team members drink coffee. John complains that he has too much to do.

2. **Look for and take shortcuts.** There is usually more than one way to complete a task. Try to find the best way and the one that takes the least amount of time.

   a. Could you get people to come to see you instead of taking the extra time to go to see them? Would a phone call or e-mail suffice?

   b. Would a written message in advance of a meeting help you accomplish more in less time when you arrive?

   c. Could you set up a luncheon meeting to accomplish a business goal and still enjoy it?

   d. Could you save time by discussing the problem with an expert instead of struggling with it too long yourself?

   e. You will manage your time better if you use a little more of it to figure out the fastest route to get where you are going.

3. **Group tasks together.** If you watch a supervisor who has learned to manage time well, you will discover that little jobs and tasks are grouped together so that they can be accomplished at the same time.

   Sometimes a manager has developed the skill to do more than one thing at the same time without offending others. When stalled on the telephone, the supervisor might read some official publications; a business matter might be introduced while walking to another meeting; when a dull staff meeting is tied up on a problem that does not involve the supervisor, he or she might plan a priority list for the next day.

   a. Maintain a list of points to cover with each person you call so that you can cover all topics in one phone call instead of several phone calls.

   b. Schedule appointments in the field to coincide with other activities away from the office.

   c. Delay a trip or meeting until it can accomplish more than one thing.

   d. Schedule conference calls.

   e. Use "meeting memos"—memos that share information in place of a meeting.

   f. A list can be made in advance so that a planning meeting will cover everything and make a follow-up unnecessary.

4. **Cut down on interruptions.** To manage your time effectively, it is often necessary to keep others from using up time that is critical to your performance. The following list offers three ways to manage interruptions.

a. Respect other people's time. When you do, you send an unspoken message that you prefer not to interrupt others and would appreciate the same treatment in return.

b. Indicate availability. Let people know when interruptions are okay. Schedule blocks of time when you are free for visits.

c. Decline to be interrupted. When someone asks "Have you got a minute?" say "Not at this time because I'm in a deadline situation. I'll get back to you when time permits." If you do it in a pleasant voice, no one should be offended. Be sure to get back to them as you said you would.

5. **Make few if any mistakes.**

a. Remember the old saying, "do it right the first time." Undoing mistakes takes time. Customer complaints and employee grievances that could have been avoided are mistakes that can eat up time voraciously. Team members who are well trained make fewer mistakes than untrained ones make. Do not be the supervisor who says, "We don't have time to train."

b. Use all the resources surrounding you to avoid mistakes or to undo them. Seek out help and advice of experienced fellow supervisors. Collectively, they possess a valuable pool of knowledge. Tap into it.

MAKE MEETINGS MORE EFFICIENT

Most managers find that it is important to have short staff meetings on a regular basis. Such meetings provide an excellent opportunity to introduce changes, solicit input, explain, and ask questions.

Staff meetings can dissipate tensions, improve relationships, communicate an important message quickly, and result in increased productivity. If not conducted properly, however, staff meetings can waste time.

Here are some simple tips to organize your meeting to reduce wasted time and increase the chances for a productive meeting:

- Have a specific goal or purpose to accomplish and announce it before you begin the meeting. Use a written agenda to organize the meeting.

- Attendees need to have the written meeting agenda well in advance of the meeting.

- Keep the meeting as short as possible. Follow the agenda and start and stop the meeting on time.

- Use care in selecting the location of the meeting to avoid distractions and interruptions.

- If a group decision is involved, get as much participation as possible. Seek alternatives to any decision proposed so that the final decision is the best one.

- Keep the meeting upbeat and energetic, and keep it moving.

- Invoke a little laughter.

- Use the meeting to demonstrate your skills in listening, summarizing information, and time management.

- Evaluate the effectiveness of your meeting so that you can do even better the next time.

- Agenda items not covered in the allotted time should be moved to the next meeting agenda.

TIME WASTERS

Your time must be managed if you are to make the most of it. Time is a finite thing. We only have 168 hours in a week in which to do all the necessary things to achieve a balanced, fulfilling life. Most full-time jobs take from 40 to 60 hours of the 168-hour total. How well we schedule and use that amount of time has a large impact on the quality of our work and nonwork lives. If you find yourself frustrated and tired because you cannot seem to accomplish what is required, you may need to organize you time in a more efficient way. This is accomplished by eliminating time wasters.

Time can be wasted in very creative ways. Some of us are very good at it. A popular way is procrastination. Putting things off until later becomes a fine art for some. Another time waster is looking for things that you use often. Put things back in their proper places. Organize your office so you can find what you need, whether a file or a piece of equipment. Searching for a misplaced item eats up time.

Misplacing or losing important reports, messages, and other paperwork is a real time waster. A good rule to follow is to handle a piece of paper only once after it is sorted. It sounds easy, but it is often difficult. For example, if a report that needs completing immediately comes across your desk, do it now. Don't sort it and place it back on your pile to be handled later. If it is a lengthy report or assignment, see if all or part of it can be delegated. Sort your mail by importance. If unimportant mail, like junk mail, finds your desk, throw it away after sorting; don't put it on top of the important report you have put off doing. Time management is worthy of your attention. Take a class, watch a video, or read a book about how to manage your time more effectively.

Analyzing your time management skills is a good place to start. Complete the Time Waster Assessment Scale on page 188.

As you organize your time at work, keep in mind that in controlling your time more effectively you do not want to squeeze all the joy out of your job. Your goal is to use your time wisely so that you will enjoy your job more, not less.

CONCLUSION

Setting priorities and managing time can enhance the quality of your life at work and at home. Managing your time effectively leaves you with more energy to do the things important to you and others. Supervisors who manage their time will set an example for their team members to follow. Working in an environment where time is wasted is frustrating.

TIME WASTER ASSESSMENT SCALE		
Instructions: Circle the number that best describes your situation or work habits.		
My office is a mess and I continually search for things.	5 4 3 2 1	My office is neat and I can find things quickly.
I am a procrastinator.	5 4 3 2 1	I establish due dates and finish on time.
I try and do it all.	5 4 3 2 1	I delegate as many tasks as I can.
I make a lot of mistakes.	5 4 3 2 1	I do things correctly the first time.
I like interruptions.	5 4 3 2 1	I schedule my day to minimize interruptions.
I keep appointments and meetings in my head.	5 4 3 2 1	I keep a detailed calendar of all appointments and due dates.
I look for opportunities to socialize whether or not I have work to do.	5 4 3 2 1	I get my work done first, then socialize.
I never plan.	5 4 3 2 1	I take time to review what needs to be done and schedule time to do them.
Scoring: Total your points. If you scored more than 20 points, there is room for improvement.		

Time management is a skill that can be learned. Tips like prioritizing activities, making lists, developing a game plan, leading meetings, evaluating how you use time, and studying time management concepts can help supervisors gain control of their time and life.

DISCUSSION QUESTIONS

1. State the benefit of setting priorities.

2. What advantages might come from keeping a priority list on a computer instead of a personal notebook? What are the disadvantages of keeping your list on the computer?

3. What is the relationship between setting long-term goals and setting daily priorities?

4. How can managing your time better improve the productivity of your team members?

5. What are your biggest time wasters? What can you do to minimize/eliminate these?

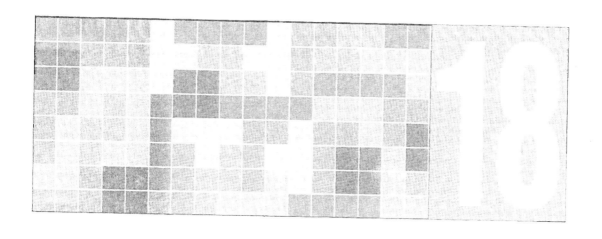

Being a
Problem Solver

Team members we work with every day will pay less attention to our decisions and more attention to the repercussions of our decisions. Our decisions must transform into action. Our action must transform into positive benefits for those we serve.

—The Authors

After you have finished reading this chapter, you should be able to

■ describe four ways to make decisions,

■ describe the group decision-making model and explain when it should be used,

■ identify the different types and levels of problems you may encounter as a supervisor, and

■ discuss the circumstances that would cause you to bring a problem to your supervisor.

THREE APPROACHES TO PROBLEM SOLVING

As a supervisor, you will find that each day a constant variety of large and small problems will come to you from all directions. You might use one of the following three approaches in dealing with them:

1. **You can stall or delay action through any number of often-used ploys.** For example, you can bury the problem in red tape, shuffle it in a circle until it disappears, overconsult with your boss until he tells you to forget it, or simply procrastinate until (you hope) a decision is no longer necessary. Using this ineffective approach will doom you to failure. Not only will you lose the respect of your superiors, you also will kill the productivity of your team members. The very nature of your job forces you to become a decision maker, and there is no escape from the responsibility. You will be expected to make good decisions, but good or bad, they must be made. Except in unusual cases, stalling or delaying will only compound the original problem.

2. **You can temporarily dispose of your problems by making quick, superficial decisions with little or no thinking and even less logic.** If you adopt this approach, you will do the following:

   a. Use your hunches instead of your logic.

   b. Refuse to consider side effects.

   c. Give each problem (large or small) the same off-the-cuff treatment.

   d. Violate the concentration techniques you learned in Chapter 17. If you take this road, you will create more problems than you solve. You will survive for a while, but in the end, you will drown in your own confusion.

3. **You can be professional in your approach and learn to solve your many problems through sound decision-making practices.** This means following a system, using logical steps, and thinking. It is not easy, but it is the only way you can make decisions that will contribute to greater departmental productivity and be accepted enthusiastically by the people who work for you. This, in turn, will build a good reputation for you with management.

EFFECTIVE DECISION MAKING

Effectively solving problems depends on sound decision making. There are basically four ways to make a decision, and all are appropriate to use when solving problems.

1. The autocratic decision is one that you make by yourself. You do not consult anyone, and you accept full responsibility for the consequences of your decision.

2. The democratic decision requires a vote to be taken on alternatives.

3. Consultative decisions involve talking about the problem with another person, perhaps a more experienced manager. Two heads are frequently better than one when a serious decision must be made. It is foolish to make a poor decision on your own if an expert is available to help you make a better one.

4. The group decision involves the entire team. If the team participates in making the decision, it will satisfy them and motivate them more. This approach would be the only acceptable process in a true team operation.

GROUP DECISION-MAKING MODEL

The following group decision-making model is an effective model for group decision making. The supervisor, acting as facilitator, with an appointed recorder from the group, follows the model. It is ideal for fostering group consensus.

1. **Communicate the situation to the group.** Openly discuss the need for a decision. Decisions are often needed when changes are being considered, so this is a good time to differentiate between "how things are now" from "how things should be."

   Maintain an open atmosphere in which questions, concerns, and perceptions about the situation can be explored. In this step, it is important that everyone understand why a decision is being considered.

2. **Brainstorm all possible decisions.** As a group, with the recorder writing on a flip chart or white board, generate as many ideas as possible. Be creative. Do not evaluate or choose any one decision at this time. Let the ideas flow.

3. **Evaluate the list of possible decisions.** Examine the idea list generated and begin to evaluate the pros and cons of each item. Evaluate the alternatives by asking at least three questions. The answers to these questions are the criteria for the selection, and they become the justification for your choice.

   Question 1: Will the choice improve the situation or solve the problem? What is the probability that we will achieve our desired state or goal?

   Question 2: Will the choice meet the needs of those involved in carrying out the decision and will those involved in implementing the decision be motivated to carry it through to completion?

Question 3: Do we, as a group, have the resources (time, money, and expertise) to carry out the decision; if not, how much help will we require from others not in our group?

Asking these questions for each alternative will eliminate some ideas immediately. Others will look good and be put on a short list of possibilities for reevaluation.

4. **Choose the best alternative.** Do not rush into a decision. It is best to postpone a decision when more discussion is needed. Be sure everyone buys in. It also is useful to ask everyone whether they are motivated to carry out the decision. If the answer is no, start over.

5. **Develop an implementation strategy.** The decision of the group must be put into action. Clarify and organize the timed, sequenced series of steps (objectives) needed for implementing the decision. This step is best left for another meeting. Allowing your group time to think about how they will implement the decision will help in the long run, but schedule an implementation meeting soon.

6. **Follow up.** Evaluate the effects of the decision. Has the situation changed in the desired way? If so, celebrate. Also be sure to thank everyone involved personally.

Some may think that this level of participation in decision making takes too much time. It does take time, but consider it an investment. People are more motivated to carry out a decision if they have had a part in making it. Overcoming resistance to unilateral decisions takes a great deal more time in the long run.

JOB-ORIENTED PROBLEMS

The two basic kinds of job-oriented problems are minor problems that require quick answers but have little permanent influence on operations and major problems that have deep and lasting influence. Most of your decision making will deal with minor job problems that you should be able to handle on the spot. Where should this new item be stored? Which report should be completed first? Should I delegate this task or do it myself? Should I write or telephone my answer?

Low-Consequence, Work-Oriented Decisions

Most job-oriented decisions the supervisor makes are low on the consequence scale. Even a bad decision for these types of problems will have little impact on productivity or the image of the manager. Faulty low-consequence decisions are usually easy to correct. Generally speaking, minor problems can be solved immediately and then forgotten. They should be disposed of in an orderly and efficient manner without consuming too much time. The major threat with these problems is that they may become psychological hang-ups for the manager when a clear-cut decision is not obvious and, through indecision, the manager permits the problem to become a major source of frustration. This kind of distortion is a luxury the manager cannot afford. The following half-minute procedure will help you make quick, frustration-free, low-consequence decisions.

1. Take time to restate the problem and review the facts in your mind (about 10 seconds).

2. Compare the first answer you think of with at least one other possibility. Weigh one against the other and try to come up with the best choice. If a decision is not obvious, make one anyway (about 15 seconds).

3. With confidence that you have made the right decision, announce it to those involved and move on to something else (about five seconds).

It is a serious mistake to make a big thing out of a low-consequence decision. You will lose the respect of your managers and the confidence of your team members. Recognize a small problem for what it is, give it the treatment recommended here, trust your judgment, and then move on to something more important.

High-Consequence, Work-Oriented Decisions

Major problems that will have a permanent influence on your operation must be given more serious treatment and more time. These problems probably challenge existing policies or procedures or involve changes in technology, layout, design, reporting methods, procedural patterns, control systems, safety rules, or basic production methods. They are major because they touch on something basic in the department and because they probably have complicating side effects. Job-connected problems of this nature and scope deserve careful attention and your best logical thinking. When they occur, lean heavily on the group decision-making model and use these additional suggestions:

- *Avoid the temptation to make a quick decision.* Gather all the available facts even if it means making a major project out of it. Ask yourself these questions: What has been done in the past? Why isn't it working today? Will a new system or approach work better? What is the real source of the problem? What are the other factors? Write down all these facts so that you clearly see the detailed overall picture.

- *If you decide to make an autocratic decision, write down and study each possible solution.* Slowly eliminate those that do not conform to company policy or have side effects that might do more damage than good. Reduce the list to the two or three possibilities that offer the best permanent solution.

- *If a clear choice is not evident, use the consultative decision approach.* Ask your superior or a key team member to talk over the remaining solutions. Sometimes possibilities need to be talked over so that the person making the decision can compare one solution with another.

- *After some careful weighing, choose the solution you feel is best and take it to your immediate supervisor for his or her reaction and approval.* Tell your supervisor why you made the decision and what results you expect. If approved, take the time to communicate the decision to all the people involved.

■ *Follow up.* Evaluate the effectiveness of the decision. Is the problem solved? Did the decision lead to a desired state?

Major job-connected problems should not be solved in haste or under pressure. When they occur, slow down and follow the logical steps outlined here.

PEOPLE-ORIENTED PROBLEMS

Low-Consequence People Problems

The most important thing you can learn about decision making is that people problems are quite different from job problems and they demand special treatment. Job-connected problems deal with tangibles or procedures that influence people; people-connected problems deal with the individuals themselves—their disappointments, frustrations, emotions, hostilities, and personality conflicts.

People problems may stem from job problems, but they exist primarily inside the team member. Approaching these issues requires your most sensitive handling. Success depends both on making a fair decision and on the way you work with the people involved.

People problems fall into two categories:

1. simple team member requests that require only limited decision making (i.e., "can I go on break?"), and

2. deep-seated, complicated problems that require considerable time and all the skill you can muster (i.e., "I'm afraid to go home, can you help me?").

Supervisors often receive special requests from team members concerning work schedules, procedures, breaks, and personal matters that are important to the individual but relatively insignificant to the operations. In most cases, you can listen carefully and give an on-the-spot yes or no answer within a few seconds without spending a great deal of time and effort. To play it safe, however, ask yourself these three questions before answering such requests:

1. Is there a written policy that governs such requests? If so, it should apply (except in unusual cases) and should be carefully explained to the team member.

2. Will granting the request damage relationships with other team members in your operations? If so (except in unusual cases), it should be refused and the reasons made clear to the person making the request.

3. Will granting the request seriously endanger the health and safety of others? If so, it should be refused and the reasons given.

When a special request does not violate any company policy, damage the supervisor's relationship with others, or endanger the safety of others, it should be granted graciously and quickly.

High-Consequence People Problems

Any people problems other than simple requests should be considered as high-consequence problems. They fall into two classifications:

1. **Those pertaining to one individual.** These problems are usually highly personal and psychological and should concern the supervisor only because they influence productivity (i.e., "My babysitter moved, I need to work days now.").

2. **Those that involve two or more team members.** These often involve friction in the relation between two or more team members and usually affect productivity (i.e., "Why do I have to work with Bob? He is slow and nobody likes him.").

Six tips to follow when solving people problems:

■ *Listen carefully to all problems or complaints.* If something is important to one of your team members, it is also important to you. Do not ignore or belittle any problem, no matter how trivial it may seem at the beginning.

■ *People problems usually involve two or more individuals, so always make an effort to gather information from all sides.* Do not take sides while you are gathering the facts.

■ *Weigh all the facts carefully before you make a decision.* Ask yourself these questions:
   ❑ Will the decision be fair to all concerned?
   ❑ Will it violate any company personnel policies?
   ❑ Do any potential serious side effects need consideration?
   ❑ Will the decision violate any human relations principles? Write down two or three possible decisions for careful evaluation before you choose one.

■ *Use effective counseling techniques. Openly communicate to all parties involved in your decision.*

■ *Take time.* Encourage a two-way conversation. Listen to any negative reactions, but stand firm on your decision.

■ *Follow up.* Work to restore or rebuild any relationships that may have been temporarily injured because of your decision.

DECISIONS AND CONSEQUENCES

Most decisions a supervisor makes basically will have one of three outcomes:

1. **Your decision improves the situation.** If your decision improves the situation, you must evaluate its effectiveness to make sure that the problem has been solved. Sometimes a decision may only address certain aspects of the problem and not totally solve it.

2. **Your decision makes the situation worse.** If your decision makes the situation worse, you must immediately take action. New decisions have to be made.

3. **Your decision will have no effect on the situation.** If your decision has no effect, you must immediately reevaluate the problem. You must analyze the situation again to determine what went wrong when you tried to address it before and how can you successfully address it now.

DECISION EMPOWERMENT

Supervisors are responsible for the activities of their team. This responsibility is not something one can relinquish—not even when you empower someone to make a decision on your behalf. Allowing others to make decisions can be motivating. It can help them develop their decision-making skills.

Follow these suggestions if you empower team members to make decisions on your behalf.

- *Make sure the team members know your expectations.* Although the decision-making power may now reside with the team member, you need to establish the parameters for which decisions are made. If you fail to set parameters, you fail to give guidance to the team member on how to meet your expectations.

- *Empower the team members with the authority to carry out decisions they are charged with making.* Nothing good will happen if team members try to carry out a decision without authority, especially if it involves other co-workers. You have to show your support and endorsement of the team members you charge with decision-making power.

- *Accept responsibility for the decisions your team members make.* Remember, they are acting on your behalf. If you are pleased with the decision your team members make, let them know. Sharing your satisfaction builds team member confidence and reinforces the decision. If you are not satisfied with the decision, accept responsibility for their action. This is a learning opportunity. Train team members on your point of view; help them understand your way of thinking.

WHEN TO SEND IT TO THE NEXT LEVEL

There will be times when you need to involve your supervisor in decisions you are making. Two situations will require your supervisor's involvement:

1. Your supervisor should hear from you on things you do that affect him or her. Informing your supervisor of your activities and giving him or her the opportunity to confirm your activities builds confidence and trust. Most supervisors will set up systems for communicating with them. In the beginning of a new relationship, you may feel like you are overcommunicating information to your supervisor. This most likely is a temporary situation.

2. If you are not certain how to handle a situation, ask your supervisor; seek advice from those with experience. This is an opportunity for you to learn.

Your supervisor also will appreciate it if you do your homework before contacting him or her. Think through your decision and how it affected or could affect the problem. Have the facts organized in your mind. Better yet, write them down. Asking your supervisor's advice regarding your decision gives your supervisor the opportunity to confirm your activities, teach you, and build your confidence and trust.

CONCLUSION

As a supervisor, you will find that each day brings a variety of large and small problems. They will come from all directions. Effectively solving problems depends on sound decision making. The group decision-making model is an effective model for group decision making. Most of your decision making will deal with minor job problems that you should be able to handle on the spot. The most important thing you can learn about decision making is that people problems are quite different from job problems and they demand special treatment. Any people problems other than simple requests should be considered as high-consequence problems. Allowing others the opportunity to make decisions is motivating. Involvement in making decisions will develop the decision-making skills of every team member.

DISCUSSION QUESTIONS

1. Why do some beginning supervisors find it so difficult to make even minor low-consequence decisions?

2. Challenge or defend the practice of dividing decisions into two categories: job oriented and people oriented.

3. Do most supervisors involve their team members in the decision-making process as much as they should? If not, why don't they?

4. Identify the steps you would take to empower a team member to make decisions on your behalf. Be specific.

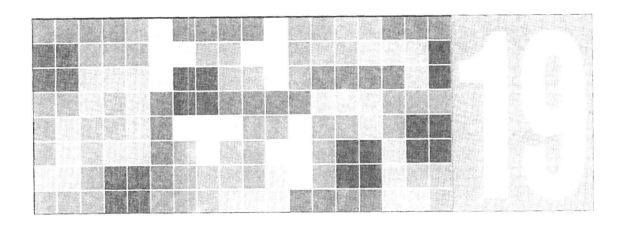

Dealing with Change and Resistance to Change

It is perfectly normal for team members to react differently to change. Some resist, some embrace it.

After you have finished reading this chapter, you should be able to

- discuss the challenges of implementing change in the workplace,

- identify the six stages of change, and

- determine effective strategies to deal with resistors of change.

STAGES OF CHANGE

Anytime you experience change, professional or personal, you will go through various mental stages of acceptance or resistance. In total, there are six stages you may go through, but you don't necessarily experience all six each time you make a change; the number is determined by your commitment to the change. The six stages are

Stage 1: Status quo

Stage 2: Resistance

Stage 3: Confusion

Stage 4: Valley of despair

Stage 5: Integration

Stage 6: Acceptance

Stage 1: Status Quo

Every change begins at the stage known as status quo. When you are in the status quo stage you are in your comfort zone; you are doing what you have become accustom to doing. You work a routine and you know what to expect. Change

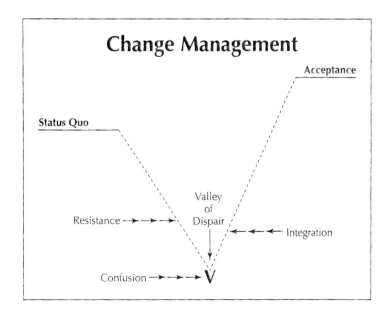

forces you to leave the status quo. Whether change is announced or unannounced, you are likely to experience Stage 2—resistance.

Stage 2: Resistance

Team members resent change because they love the comfort of the status quo; they don't normally understand the need for the change. A common mistake among hospitality supervisors is to implement change without explaining the "whys" behind it. Team members feel that if you are going to disrupt their work environment and change their routine, they are entitled to know the reasons. Explaining will help you break though the barrier of resistance.

Stages of Change

Resistance — Why? Why? Why???

Sometimes, even after hearing the reasons behind a change, some team members will reject it. As far as they are concern, whatever has been working will continue to work and there is no need to change. Notice that we said that *some* team members will reject the change. When it comes to change, team members typically fall into one of three categories:

1. **Change friendly.** These team members are small in numbers. They are the ones you typically rely on to carry out directives. When you ask them to do something, they respond without reservation, hesitation, or questions. They simply do what you need to have done because you asked them.

2. **Uncommitted or neutral.** Being uncommitted or neutral does not mean that team members are against the change. It does mean that people are unsure that the change is necessary. They want proof. This group can be influenced to become change friendly or to hate change. Provide the proof they seek and this group easily can become adaptable.

3. **Resistors.** This group of team members will deliberately try to make the change fail. Some team members resist because they believe that change is an inquisition on the way they work . Some team members resist because they feel

that change imposes on their freedom at work. Others resist because they think all change is bad, and still others resist because they don't like you. No matter what reason they have for resisting, these team members will oppose change.

Typical Breakdown of Team Members' Resistance

Breakdown of team loyalty

- 30% of team members are change friendly
- 50% of team members are "neutral"—uncommitted

These team members are on the fence in a so-called neutral position, trying to figure out which way to lean. Not hostile to change, but they're not helping like they should.

- **20% of team members hate the change and are deliberately trying to make the change fail.**

Source: Research data collected by author, unpublished.

If you announced a change to your team, which group is more likely to speak out against the change? You are correct if you said the third group. Team members who hate the change will often be outspoken in their resistance. When this situation occurs, supervisors often respond to these team members by trying to convince, persuade, threaten, bribe, punish, and beg this group to adopt the change.

However, by focusing your energy and time working on the group that is against the change, you defeat the change. Remember, this group does not want the change to work. They focus on what they perceive to be its weaknesses and flaws. If this group is ignored or mishandled, they may sabotage the change by convincing other neutral team members to resist it. If this happens, 70% of your team members (50% neutral team members and 20% resistors) are now working against the change. This also creates an awkward situation for the 30% of team members who were change friendly. Even if they support the change, peer pressure may pull their support from you.

Supervisors who continually are drawn into the trap set by the resistor type team members perpetuate this cycle, and teams that resist change are vulnerable in today's world. The hospitality industry is constantly changing due to changing markets, economics conditions, and legislation; therefore, it is important for supervisors to be able to successfully negotiate change in their operations.

Types of Resistors

There are three categories of resistor team members:

- Those that call attention to themselves
- Those that disguise their resistance
- Those that sabotage change

Resistors that Call Attention to Themselves.   This group of team members resists by calling negative attention to themselves.

A change has been introduced into Tiffany's routine. She must now wear gloves. When she assembles ready-to-eat foods with her hands, her manager requires her to wear gloves. Tiffany hates wearing plastic gloves. She reluctantly wears them. The entire time Tiffany is wearing the plastic gloves you can hear her complaining throughout the kitchen.
"Why do we have to wear these gloves?"
"I hate wearing these gloves."
"These gloves make my fingers smell funny."
"I can't feel anything with these gloves on."
"These gloves don't feel right."
"The food is going to taste like plastic.
"These gloves are making me sick."

Although she is complying with the requirement of wearing plastic gloves, she draws negative attention to herself.

A typical management response to Tiffany might be to

1. Ignore Tiffany and let her rant.

2. Explain the reason she has to wear the gloves to Tiffany again.

3. Tell Tiffany to take off the gloves.

4. Tell Tiffany to wear the gloves and be quiet.

Tiffany resists change by complaining about it. As a supervisor, you should address her negative behavior.

Resistors that Disguise their Resistance.   This group of team members disguises resistance. They are smart enough to know that they have to comply with the change, but when the supervisor's attention is drawn away from them, they can go back to doing things the way it was done before the change. They disguise their resistance by doing what you want when you are watching. When you are not there to keep an eye on them, they fail to follow through on the change.

Supervisor: "Put your gloves on."
Camellia: "I keep forgetting I have to wear them."

(She puts them on, but a few minutes later, she takes them off.)

Supervisor: "Where are your gloves? Put on your gloves."
Camellia: "I had to take them off to wash my hands."

(She puts them on, but a few minutes later, she takes them off.)

Supervisor: "Where are your gloves? Put on your gloves."
Camellia: "They got dirty. I had to take them off."

(She puts them on, but a few minutes later, she takes them off.)

| Supervisor: | "Where are your gloves? Put on your gloves." |
| Camellia: | "I didn't notice I didn't have them on." |

(She puts them on, but a few minutes later, she takes them off.)

| Supervisor: | "Where are your gloves? Put on your gloves." |
| Camellia: | "I had to take them off to [fill in the blank]." |

(She puts them on, but a few minutes later, she takes them off.)

This ritual is a battle of wills. It comes down to endurance. These team members know they have to comply to avoid discipline. They also know they can push the issue to a certain point. Once you get tired of checking up on them, they can go back to doing what they want to do.

These resistors know you are busy, and they are counting on other matters diverting your attention to keep you off their backs.

Resistors that Sabotage   This group of team members creates ways to deter and/or defeat the change. Their mission is to make sure the change fails.

Josephine hates wearing plastic gloves. She shyly disposes of the entire box of gloves into the dumpster.

Supervisor:	"Put your gloves on."
Josephine:	"I don't have any."
Supervisor:	"Where are they?"
Josephine:	"I don't know."

Team members who sabotage your objectives are the most destructive type of resistor.

Resistors and Implementing Change

When you implement a change, start by explaining the "whys" behind it and work with the team members that are change friendly so that they can help successfully make the change. Once the change has been proven to work, they may help convince the neutral team members to accept it.

Now you will have 80% of your team members accepting the change (30% change-friendly team members and 50% neutral team members).[1]

The only thing left to do is deal with the resistors. You will never be able to advance the objectives of your operation successfully until you deal with the resistors. They will circumvent your efforts and taint the willingness of other team members who want to make the change succeed. Fail to deal with resistors and you will fail.

To deal effectively with resistors, you must take the following steps:

■ *Establish the rules.* Make sure all team members know what is expected. Train and evaluate team members to make sure they are capable of executing tasks related to the change, and continue to train as necessary.

[1]Research data collected by author, unpublished

- *Respond quickly.* You must confront team members that fail to perform the new tasks. Don't lower your standards to their performance; raise their performance to your standards.

- *Respond consistently.* Enforce your expectations consistently. Don't just do it sometimes.

- *Counsel and motivate.* Try to help team members adjust during the change.

- *Use progressive discipline.* Team members are adults. They are responsible for their performance. When they choose to disregard your directive, they must accept the consequences of their decision. Don't fail to do your job because team members have failed to do their jobs.

If you don't manage the resistance of team members, the change will fail, and you will return to status quo.

Stage 3: Confusion

Change can be very confusing. In this stage, team members are learning. As team members go through the change, they will experience confusion, the feeling of uneasiness and unfamiliarity that often comes with change. To survive this stage you must

- help team members focus on the behavior that supports the change,

- reiterate the goals and benefits of the change,

- reinforce training,

- praise behaviors that support the change, and

- correct behavior that doesn't support the change.

If you don't manage the confusion of team members, the change will fail and you will return to status quo.

Stage 4: Valley of Despair

Despair occurs when a person feels a sense of defeat. This can happen when team members' confidence is shaken, you grow weary from the challenge of the change, or everyone wishes it was the way it used to be.

Change is emotional. To manage despair associated with it you must

- *Become a beacon of hope.* Team members will look to you for strength and guidance.

- *Watch your words and your deeds.* If you have reservations about the change, discuss them with you supervisor, not with your team members.

- *Persevere.* Remain steadfast and committed to implementing the change.

- *Stay positive.* You cannot be successful while being negative. Negativity is contagious, so choose to be positive.

Stage 5: Integration

Integration is the process of adjusting to change. Sometimes, even after we are committed, the change itself is a problem. In this stage, we make adjustments to accomplish the change successfully. For example,

- We adopted a new register system and there was a glitch in the computer program. A patch is installed and the whole store learns new procedures to use the system.

- To offer fresher foods, the company starts making fresh cakes onsite instead of buying frozen cakes. Everyone has to learn how to make cakes from scratch.

Stage 6: Acceptance

The last stage of implementing change is acceptance. The effect of the change determines its success. The following are three change management diagrams.

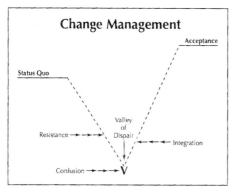

Diagram 1

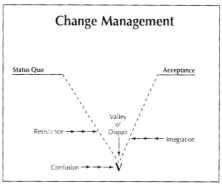

Diagram 2

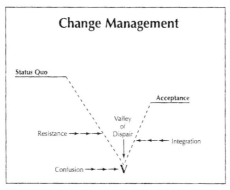

Diagram

Diagram 1 represents a "good change." Notice that the stage of acceptance is higher than that of the status quo stage. This means that implementing this change led to a higher performance/productivity.

Diagram 2 represents a neutral change. The stage of acceptance is equal to the status quo stage in this diagram; therefore, this change had no significant impact on the performance/productivity.

Diagram 3 represents a bad change. The stage of acceptance is lower than that of the status quo stage. This change had a negative impact on the performance/productivity.

CONCLUSION

Anytime you experience change, professional or personal, you will go through various mental stages of acceptance or resistance. In total, there are six stages you may go through, but you don't necessarily experience all six each time you make a change; the number is determined by your commitment to the change. Sometimes, even after hearing the reasons behind a change, some team members will reject it. As far as they are concerned, whatever has been working will continue to work and there is no need to change. When you implement a change, start by explaining the "whys" behind it and work with the team members that are change friendly so that they can help successfully make the change. Once the change has been proven to work, they may help convince the neutral team members to accept it.

DISCUSSION QUESTIONS

1. Use the stages of change to explain a challenge you are experiencing.

2. How can you minimize the impact of resistors on your organization?

3. Explain the impact of each type of resistor on your organization.

4. Explain why team members who sabotage your objectives are the most destructive element to change.

5. How can change-friendly team members help you make changes in your operation?

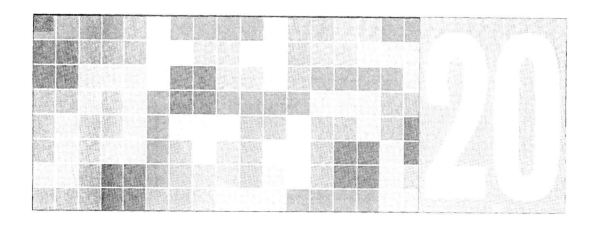

Change and
Your Opportunities
for Growth

The greatest danger for most of us is not that we aim too high and miss the mark, but that our aim is too low and we reach it.

—Author Unknown

After you have finished reading this chapter, you should be able to

- discuss why change is important for organizations,

- list examples of ways to make change less stressful for your team members,

- describe how to prepare for promotion opportunities, and

- list questions you should ask yourself when deciding whether or not to leave a company.

GROWTH AND CHANGE IN THE HOSPITALITY ENVIRONMENT

When managers use words such as *downsizing, layoffs, restructuring, relocating, decentralizing, new information technology,* and *retraining,* you know that change is around the corner. The dramatic tempo of change in the workplace continues to accelerate, and the impact falls more on the supervisor than on team members. As a beginning supervisor, the way you accept and interpret changes to your staff and how you cope personally will have a measurable effect on operational productivity and your future success.

Often an individual hears about a pending change and promptly converts it into a negative instead of an opportunity. You hear comments like these:

"They said, 'we've got to do this.'"
"There is no security in a big company anymore."
"Don't worry, give it some time, it will be back the way it was before you know it."
"This constant changing may force me into a nervous breakdown."
"Early retirement may be my solution."

How you as a supervisor cope with change will depend on your attitude. Some people have the capacity to view change as opportunity; others reject even good changes with hostility. What is your attitude toward change?

Not all changes are good or necessary. Resisting an ill-advised change can be a worthy mission that will protect and benefit your company and your team members. But most changes are inevitable, and the sooner they are accepted by you as a supervisor, the better it will be for your team members. In spite of short-term adjustment disadvantages, many changes have long-term advantages that make the adjustment worthwhile. It will be your responsibility to communicate this situation to your team members when it occurs.

Team members take their cues from their supervisor. When the supervisor openly acts out his or her disappointment or rejection of a change, team members will react accordingly. Certainly it is possible for team members to respond negatively even when you respond positively; however, their reactions are intensified when you are negative.

Supervisors who feel the need to express concerns about a change should pass their concerns on to their supervisor. Only communicating concerns to one's team members is not effective.

Technological Changes

Every facet of business—transportation, agriculture, food processing, product development, product procurement, manufacturing, banking, retailing, education, and government inspection facilities—is feeling the impact of technological change. The way we prepare foods, take orders, pay bills, train team members, take reservations, and coordinate schedules will continue to change as a result of technology.

As a management person, supervisors may be caught in the middle. When sweeping changes come from above, it is the responsibility of the supervisors to see that those who work below them accept the changes. Even more critical, supervisors may need to teach their team members new techniques and procedures so that change can take place.

Wherever you work as a supervisor, technological change will challenge your position. Technology often increases productivity and profit; you can view these changes as opportunities to prepare yourself for a higher position, or you can take a negative view and eliminate yourself from the race.

When May heard that her firm would adopt a more sophisticated computer system, her first reaction was negative. As an operations officer, she knew the change would involve substantial new responsibility for her. She would have to undergo additional training that would be difficult. Besides learning new skills, she would have to spend many hours of additional time helping her nine team members adjust. At first, she even considered changing her career, but after talking things over with her supervisor, she decided to turn the announcement into an opportunity. She said to herself, "If computers are going to dominate this industry, then I am going to dominate the computers so that I can use my skills to increase my upward mobility." She promptly enrolled in her company's training department computer course for beginners, a course that would improve her skills with computers. She also enrolled in a general course in data processing at a local college, and she welcomed the information provided by the computer firm. May was determined to take advantage of change to improve her own future. Her superiors were quick to recognize her positive attitude toward changes over which they, too, had little control.

Organizations Change to Survive

At one time in the United States, a supervisor felt lucky to work for a stable, predictable corporation. A supervisor could anticipate security and upward mobility within the framework of a single large organization. A first-line supervisor could blueprint a career path to the top with confidence, and he or she knew, at least to some extent, what was ahead.

Today, one should feel lucky to work for an organization that is sufficiently flexible to adjust to changes and survive. Organizations that are too slow to adjust will be left behind and supervisors and team members who belong to such organizations will find themselves unemployed. Cursory reviews of newspaper headlines illustrate this point almost daily.

Changes are hitting companies of all sizes with increasing magnitude. Mergers, takeovers, and staff reductions are in the headlines. You should not infer that the organization you are currently working for is so vulnerable to change that it may turn belly-up, but if your organization is not adaptable enough to survive, your job may disappear. Your attitude should be, "I'm lucky that the management of my organization is flexible enough to keep the organization alive and changing." It should not be, "I hope my organization can resist change and stay the way it is."

As a supervisor, you are in a key role to help your organization survive and prosper. You will need to be flexible enough to reorganize your operations, accept new technology and assignments, and, most of all, assist your team members in making their adjustment.

> Doug couldn't understand why his hotel needed to make changes. As a result, he resisted what few changes were made and refused to learn new techniques that were revolutionizing his particular career area. Because of inflexible, shortsighted management, his hotel went into bankruptcy, and Doug was left out on a limb. His failure to learn new techniques left him unprepared for a similar job. He had contributed to the demise of his organization and permitted himself to become obsolete in his career specialty.

Workforce Changes

The U.S. workforce has been changing rapidly during the last 10 years; it is becoming more multicultural and multilingual. Women have moved into all occupations and are making faster progress up executive ladders. African Americans, Hispanics, Asians, and a growing number of people from other cultures are improving their skills, earning greater upward mobility, and creating change in our industry. The new workforce is a challenge to the front-line supervisor because it is he or she who must work with all individuals on a personal, one-to-one basis.

> Ten years ago, Herbert had 20 team members in his operation: 17 white males, two white females, and one African American male. Today, thanks to his human relations skills, productivity is higher with only 16 team members. The composition is as follows: five white females, four white males, two African American males, two Asians females, one African American female, one Hispanic male, and one Hispanic female. Herbert takes pride in the cultural mix of his operation. From the start, he accepted the change as a personal challenge and enjoyed helping the few remaining senior team members in his operation adjust.

CHANGE AS A SOURCE OF STRESS

Supervisors who establish realistic goals, maintain comfortable priorities, and manage their time are in a position to balance their careers with their personal lives. This balance helps prevent burnout when things are stable. When major changes occur, they always introduce stress; the perceptive supervisor is prepared for temporary adjustments until career and home are again properly balanced. A balanced, happy, activity-centered, relaxing home life is one of the best insurances against stress generated in the workplace.

Team member stress comes from many sources: work overload, role conflicts, over-supervision, ambiguity, insecurity, and change. Although you want to protect your team members from such pressures, you cannot provide a 100% stress-free work environment. In fact, mild positive stress (eustress) stimulates greater productivity. Some work environments, such as restaurants, convention centers, amusement parks, and sport arenas, have built-in stress. The way you handle change in your operation, however, can eliminate a great deal of harmful stress (distress) that might injure team members and eat away at productivity standards.

To convert negatives into positives, you should portray changes as opportunities for growth instead of problems to overcome. You should communicate such changes in a nonthreatening way as far in advance as possible so that team members have time to adjust. You also should explain why such changes are necessary. Team members who participate in the planning of change experience a reduction in the stress that change can bring.

As you accomplish these goals, consider the following suggestions:

■ Turn change into opportunity for yourself. When it comes to change, it doesn't hurt to think of yourself first because if you don't succeed, those working for you will be left unprepared. It is bad enough to work for a supervisor who is negative about change; it is even worse to work for one who neglects to prepare you for the future.

■ Communicate the advantages of change. Tell your staff that changing now may save their jobs later. State that the way to protect their retirement pensions in the future is to reach for greater profitability now. Communicate this message individually, in staff meetings, and during formal appraisal periods. Prepare your people to anticipate change and learn to roll with the punches. You will be doing them an immense favor.

■ Participating in the planning of change is motivating for those affected by the change. As much as possible, allow your team members to be involved in the change. Ask their opinion about how to implement changes. Keep them informed as the changes are discussed by upper management.

■ Provide team members with ongoing, continuous advanced training. Frequently, highly capable persons take their skills with them to a new company or community only to discover that their competencies are obsolete. Do not let obsolescence happen to your staff. Provide them with the kind of training they need to stay up to date with career demands where they are or where they move in the future. Allowing your staff to rest on their career laurels is doing them a disservice.

■ When one accepts the premise that change is inevitable, it is possible to take pride in being able to cope with change effectively. Anything you can do to help your team members experience this pride will make you a superior supervisor.

PREPARING FOR YOUR NEXT PROMOTIONAL OPPORTUNITY

The hospitality industry offers real opportunities for any supervisor willing to step up to the challenge. Even during times of economic carnage, the hospitality industry continues to expand and provide career opportunities for every level of leadership. The lodging component of the hospitality industry alone will add more than 60,000 new rooms this year. What does all this growth mean? Opportunities for well-trained supervisors.

Learning and doing the job that will become your next promotion is a matter of preparation. Here are just a few things you should be doing:

- *Build alliances outside of your company.* You need to have people you can go to outside of your company to help you. You need to have people in your life who care about you and will be honest with you. People who are honest enough to tell you the truth about yourself. People who are willing to tell you the good news and the hard-to-hear news you need to be told. We all have things we can improve about ourselves; having people in your life that care about you will keep you moving in the right direction.

- *Most opportunities are not published.* It is a powerful asset to know whom you can seek out for assistance when considering opportunities to improve yourself.

- *Build your internal network.* Seek out the people within your company who can help you become better at what you do. Look for the individuals who are in a position to help you. Become known in your company as an achiever, helper, contributor, and team player.

- *Continue your education.* Never stop learning. Never stop growing. The easiest and best thing you can do is read. Your best ideas can come from reading. Expand your knowledge and you expand your abilities to handle problems and think on a higher tier. Read trade publications. Read development books. Just read! Your education should never stop.

- *Do your homework.* Learn what you have to know and do to be ready for your next position.

- *Do your job.* Your performance in your current position is the best indicator of what your performance will be in your new position. Don't be so busy pursuing your next job that you fail to do the job you are currently employed to do.

Good jobs, great people, extraordinary opportunity. The restaurant industry employs more than 12 million people in 878,000 locations and continues to grow. The *forecast for 2004:* $440.1 billion in sales.

Source: National Restaurant Association, 2004 Restaurant Industry Forecast Executive Summary.

■ *Improve your skills and become an expert.* Master the skills required to do your job. Then update and refine your skills. If necessary, take a class. Improve your communications, counseling, technical, time management, and organizational planning skills.

■ *Set goals.* You can't get to where you are going without a plan.

■ *Update your resume.* At the minimum you should review your credentials on a quarterly basis to make sure your resume is current.

DETERMINING WHEN IT IS TIME TO CHANGE YOUR EMPLOYER

This is a difficult subject to undertake, especially in an industry that already experiences way too much turnover in management. On one hand, we need to encourage dedication, commitment, and loyalty. On the other hand, we need not be blind to our circumstances. The rewards of employment should benefit both parties.

No one should tell you when you should leave your employer. No matter how much they may think they understand your circumstances, they are not you. What we can do is help you think through the process of determining the right course of action for yourself. Ask yourself the following questions:

■ Financial
- ❑ Does your current position satisfy your financial needs?
- ❑ Are you making enough money?
- ❑ Are you spending your money wisely? Is the problem money management?
- ❑ Is your compensation aligned with your expectations of the position?
- ❑ What alternatives do you have to bridge your financial gap other than leaving your job?
- ❑ Is this money shortfall temporary or permanent?

■ Leadership
- ❑ Can you trust your supervisor?
- ❑ Are you happy with the relationship you have with your supervisor?
- ❑ Can anything be done to improve your relationship with your supervisor? Have you told your supervisor?
- ❑ What do you like about your supervisor?
- ❑ What don't you like about your supervisor? Is this worth leaving your job?
- ❑ What would you do if your new boss manages the same way as your old boss? Can you do that now?

■ Opportunity cost
- ❑ What would you gain by leaving?
- ❑ What would you lose by leaving?
- ❑ What would you gain by staying?
- ❑ What would you lose by staying?
- ❑ What is more costly, staying or leaving?

- Pros and cons
  - ❏ What are the pros and cons of your current job?
  - ❏ What are the pros and cons of the new position?
  - ❏ Which list of cons are you willing to tolerate?

- Quality of home life versus quality of work life
  - ❏ How does your current job affect your home life?
  - ❏ Which job improves your home life?
  - ❏ If you have to choose between a better home life and a better work life, which would you choose? Which job best supports your answer?

- The people you know versus the people you don't know
  - ❏ Which group poses the greatest challenge to you?
  - ❏ Which group do you find more appealing to work with?
  - ❏ Which group is more likely to give you a fair chance?

- Tradeoffs
  - ❏ What are you willing to lose to get that next position? For how long? Then what?
  - ❏ What are you losing by staying in your current position?
  - ❏ What is the real price of leaving?

- Treatment
  - ❏ How are you treated at work?
  - ❏ How do you feel when you are at work?
  - ❏ What would make you feel better?
  - ❏ What would make you feel worse?
  - ❏ Which job has a better chance of making you feel good?

- Upward mobility
  - ❏ Which job has the best career track?
  - ❏ Which job would best help you achieve the majority of your goals?
  - ❏ What are your goals?
  - ❏ Have you looked for other opportunities in your current company? Have you talked to anybody? Does your current employer know what you want? Do you know what you want?
  - ❏ Which job will help you best in the long term?
  - ❏ How much do you really know about this other company? What proof do you have to confirm your belief? What do you need to know now that could prevent you from being in this same dilemma five years from now?

- Your happiness
  - ❏ Which job would make you feel good about yourself?
  - ❏ Which job provides you the most pleasure?

❑ Which job allows you to do what you enjoy doing?

❑ What are the little things about your current job you will miss? Is leaving worth missing these things?

■ Your health

❑ Which job will allow you to improve your health habits?

❑ Which job has the most negative stress?

❑ Which job would best support your wellness?

By taking the time to answer the preceding questions, you will be able to proceed with confidence that whatever decision you make is the right decision for you.

CONCLUSION

The dramatic tempo of change in the workplace continues to accelerate, and the impact falls more on the supervisor than on team members. As a beginning supervisor, the way you accept and interpret changes to your staff and how you cope personally will have a measurable effect on operational productivity and your future success. Team members take their cues from their supervisor. When you openly act out your disappointment or rejection of a change, team members will react accordingly. The U.S. workforce has been changing rapidly during the last 10 years; it is becoming more multicultural and multilingual.

DISCUSSION QUESTIONS

1. Can all changes be converted into opportunities? Defend your answer through examples.

2. What can supervisors do to minimize stress within themselves? For team members? Evaluate possibilities such as physical exercise and meditation.

3. Explain why change is the primary source of stress in our society.

4. Think of your own situation. How much change is in your life? How do you react to change and how might your reaction be modified to reduce stress?

5. How can you best prepare yourself for your next promotional opportunity?

6. How will you know when it is time to change jobs/companies? Explain your answer.

Appendix

Web Sites for Further Research

1.	A Closer Look	*www.a-closerlook.com*
2.	American Hotel and Lodging Association	*www.ahma.com*
3.	American Management Association	*www.amanet.org*
4.	Bartending Site	*www.behind-bars.net*
5.	CHART—Council of Hotel and Restaurant Management	*www.chart.org*
6.	Council for Hotel and Restaurant Industry	*www.chrie.org*
7.	E-Hospitality.com	www.e-hospitality.com
8.	Find a Seminar	*www.findaseminar.com*
9.	Find Articles	*www.findarticles.com*
10.	Foodservice Management	*www.ecornell.com*
11.	Hcareers.com Hospitality Industry Careers	*www.hcareers.com*
12.	Hospitality Employment	*www.chefsatwork.com*
13.	Hospitality Employment	*www.entreejobbank.com*
14.	Hospitality Employment	*www.escoffier.com*
15.	Hospitality Employment	*www.foodservice.com*

16.	Hospitality Employment	*www.gottajob.com*
17.	Hospitality Employment	*www.restaurantjobs.com*
18.	Hospitality Employment	*www.restaurantjobsnetwork.com*
19.	Hospitality Employment	*www.restaurantmanagers.com*
20.	Hospitality Employment	*www.resturantrecruit.com*
21.	Hospitality Employment	*www.starchefs.com*
22.	Hospitality Industry	*www.hospitality-industry.com*
23.	Hospitality Joblinks.com	*www.hospitalityjoblinks.com*
24.	Hospitality Magazines	*www.restaurantresults.com*
25.	Hospitality Net	*www.hospitalitynet.org*
26.	Hospitality Office	*www.hospitalityoffice.com*
27.	Hospitality Online	*www.hospitalityonline.com*
28.	Hotel and Motel Management Online	*www.hotelmotel.com*
29.	Hotel Online	*www.hotel-online.com*
30.	Hotel Resource	*www.hotelresource.com*
31.	Hotel Training	*www.hoteltraining.com*
32.	International Hotel and Restaurant Association	*www.ih-ra.com*
33.	Multicultural Foodservice and Hospitality Alliance	*www.mfha.net*
34.	National Restaurant Association— Education Foundation	*www.nraef.org*
35.	National Restaurant Association	*www.restaurant.org*
36.	Resource Center for Workforce Solutions	*www.nraef.org/solutions*
37.	Restaurant News	*www.smartbrief.com*
38.	Restaurant Operators (Training)	*www.restaurantowner.com*
39.	Restaurant Report	*www.restaurantreport.com*
40.	Restaurant Workshop	*www.restaurantworkshop.com*
41.	Restaurant.com	*www.restaurant.com*
42.	Staffing Resources	*www.thesauce.com*
43.	Team Member Motivation	*www.billmain.com*
44.	Team Member Motivation	*www.eaward.com*
45.	Team Member Motivation	*www.employer-employee.com*
46.	Team Member Motivation	*www.generationsatwork.com*
47.	Woman's Foodservice Forum	*www.womensfoodserviceforum.com*

Index